Karl Zimmermann, Andrew Dickson White, Martin Luther, Georgiana Malcolm

Luther's Letters to Women

Karl Zimmermann, Andrew Dickson White, Martin Luther, Georgiana Malcolm
Luther's Letters to Women
ISBN/EAN: 9783337127053
Printed in Europe, USA, Canada, Australia, Japan
Cover: Foto ©Lupo / pixelio.de

More available books at **www.hansebooks.com**

LUTHER'S

LETTERS TO WOMEN.

Collected by

DR. K. ZIMMERMANN.

Translated by

MRS. MALCOLM.

LONDON:
CHAPMAN AND HALL, 193 PICCADILLY.

1865.

LONDON:
LEVEY AND CO., PRINTERS, GREAT NEW STREET,
FETTER LANE, E.C.

PREFACE.

THESE Letters of Luther, collected by Dr. K. Zimmermann, and given by him as a Whitsuntide offering to the German Protestant woman-world, I now present as a Christmas gift to the women of England.

Among them a few, perhaps, may be looked upon as trifling, others as curious and interesting, whilst some are beautiful; but all bear testimony to the simple, earnest faith, deep piety, and loving heart of this great and good man, showing how his religion was interwoven with his every-day life, and that his family affections were particularly strong. His Will has been introduced by Dr. Zimmermann as a further proof "that the man who stood at the head of his time did not forget his household ties."

In Luther's character were marvellously combined the most opposite qualities—dignity and earnestness with simplicity and playfulness; bitterness and severity with long-suffering and charity; sternness with gentleness and tenderness. There may occasionally be found in the Letters a certain degree of coarseness; which must not be regarded as peculiar to Luther, but as belonging to the times in which he lived.

I venture to bring this little book before the English public in the hope that it may prove of some use, in this age of weak and wavering faith, by recalling to the memory, the character and writings of one who has left so bright an example of the power of that steadfast faith which is " the victory that overcometh the world."

CONTENTS.

LETTER		PAGE
I.	To Margaret Duchess of Brunswick	1
II.	To three banished Court Damsels	4
III.	To a Noble Lady in a Convent	8
IV.	To some Nuns	10
V.	To Katherine Schützin	14
VI.	To Maria Queen of Hungary	16
VII.	To Frau Dorothea Jörger	21
VIII.	To Else von Kanitz	23
IX.	To Elizabeth, Wife of Agricola	25
X.	To Frau Felicitas von Selmenitz	27
XI.	To Margaret N.	29
XII.	To Frau Goritzin	32
XIII.	To his Wife	33
XIV.	To Katherine Hornung	37
XV.	To the Wife of J. Jonas	40
XVI.	To his Wife	42
XVII.	To his Wife	44
XVIII.	To his Wife	47
XIX.	To the Wife of Matthew Zell	49
XX.	To Barbara Lischnerin	51

LETTER		PAGE
XXI.	To his Mother	57
XXII.	To his Wife	64
XXIII.	To Frau Dorothea Jörger	68
XXIV.	To Frau von Stockhausen	71
XXV.	To Frau Jörger	73
XXVI.	To Frau Jörger	75
XXVII.	To the Abbess of Hervord, in Westphalia. Written together with Melancthon	78
XXVIII.	To Frau Jörger	81
XXIX.	To his Wife	83
XXX.	To an Unknown Person	85
XXXI.	To Frau Jörger	87
XXXII.	To the same	89
XXXIII.	To the same	91
XXXIV.	To his Wife	93
XXXV.	To an Unknown Person	95
XXXVI.	To the Duchess Elizabeth of Brunswick	97
XXXVII.	To Ursula Schneidewin, at Stollberg	99
XXXVIII.	To the same	102
XXXIX.	To the Duchess Katherine of Saxony	105
XL.	To Dorothea, the Wife of B. Mackenrot, at Rossla, Luther's Sister	107
XLI.	To the Duchess Elizabeth of Brunswick	109
XLII.	To the Duchess Katherine of Saxony	111
XLIII.	To his Wife	113

LETTER		PAGE
XLIV.	To the same	115
XLV.	To the same	117
XLVI.	Luther's Will	118
XLVII.	To the Widow of J. Cellarius	124
XLVIII.	To one unknown	126
XLIX.	To the Electress Elizabeth of Brandenburg	130
L.	To the same	131
LI.	To the Electress Sibylla of Saxony	133
LII.	To the same	136
LIII.	To the Wife of Jerome Baumgärtner, at Nuremberg	138
LIV.	To Frau Jörger	142
LV.	To the same	144
LVI.	To the Widow of George Schulzen	146
LVII.	To an Aged Couple	148
LVIII.	To his Wife	151
LIX.	To the same	154
LX.	To the same	156
LXI.	To the same	158
LXII.	To the same	160
LXIII.	To the same	164
LXIV.	To the same	166

Luther's Letters to Women.

LETTER I.

To Margaret Duchess of Brunswick.
December 1519.

Luther dedicates to the Duchess, who was very favourable to the new religious movement, some writings, which in the letter he calls sermons.

To my gracious lady, her Serene Highness and high-born Princess Frau Margaretta, born Von Ritberze, Duchess of Brunswick and Luneburg, I, Martin Luther, Augustiner at Wittenberg, by the help of all God's good gifts to me, present God's grace and peace in Christ our Lord.

HIGH-BORN Princess and gracious Lady,—some of my good friends, Fathers and Superiors, have suggested to me to dedicate something spiritual and Christian to your Princely Grace, that I may thus thankfully acknowledge the gracious condescension and favour that your Princely Grace shows towards my unworthy self, and thus tender you my humble service. To this I have often felt bound in duty, yet have been deterred by the feeling of my own insufficiency to fulfil this desire and duty, especially as I hold it certain that our Master, Christ, has been beforehand with me in the instruction of your Princely Grace. I have, however, at last allowed myself to be moved by your Princely Grace's devotion to the Holy Scriptures, of which I have heard much, to cause to be dedicated to your Princely Grace some sermons on the holy, venerated, and comfortable sacraments of Repentance,[1] of Baptism,[2] and of the most sacred Body;[3] seeing that there are so many troubled and anxious consciences, as I myself have experienced, who do not recognise the

[1] Walch, *Luther's Works*, x. p. 1478.
[2] *Id.* x. p. 2592.
[3] *Id.* xix. p. 522. Zimmermann, *Luther's Reform Writings*, i. p. 392.

holy and full grace of the sacraments, nor know how to avail themselves of them; but endeavour presumptuously to satisfy themselves with their own works, rather than seek God's favour and peace in the holy sacraments. Thus, by man's teaching, the holy sacraments have been veiled and withdrawn from us. I beg your Princely Highness will graciously accept this my small service, and not be angry at my presumption; for I am at all times ready submissively to serve your Princely Grace, whom I commend to God both here and hereafter. Amen.

LETTER II.

To three banished Court Damsels.
June 18, 1523.

Duke Henry of Saxony, though not himself unfavourable to the Reformer, had, from fear of his brother Duke George, Luther's mortal enemy, banished three Court damsels, because Luther's writings had been found in their possession. On hearing this, Luther sends them this letter of comfort.

To the honourable, virtuous damsels Hannah von Draschwitz, Milia von Olsnitz, and Ursula von Feilitzin, my special friends in Christ.

GRACE and peace in Christ to you, honourable, virtuous, and dear damsels. Herr Nicholas von Amsdorf[1] has acquainted me with the trouble and contumely that you

---

[1] Nicholas von Amsdorf was one of the first and most zealous adherents of Luther. After being professor at Wittenberg, he became superintendent at Magdeburg, then Bishop of Naumburg. He died superintendent at Eisenach.

have experienced at the court at Freiberg[1] on account of my books, and has also desired me to write you a letter of consolation. Although I consider you do not require comfort from me,—and am, besides, disinclined to write to persons unknown to me,—yet I did not know how to refuse him.

In the first place, it is my earnest request that you will set your hearts at rest, and neither do nor wish any thing evil to those who have ill-used you. As St. Paul teaches, in the 4th chap. Corinthians, 12th verse,—"Being reviled, we bless." Also, Christ says, in Matthew, 5th chap. 44th verse, "Bless them that curse you; do good to them that hate you; and pray for them which despitefully use you and persecute you." Thus do, considering that you are enlightened by the grace of God, and they are blind and stubborn; also that they do more injury to their own souls than all the world can do to them. You are, indeed, only too well revenged on them for acting unjustly towards you, as thus they rage and horribly rebel against God:

[1] The Duke's court was held at Freiberg.

it is rather fitting that you should pity them as mad, unthinking men, who do not see how deplorably they ruin themselves when they think to do you an injury. Wait, and let Christ act; He will richly recompense your disgrace, and raise you higher than you could wish, if you will only leave all to Him.

And even if you should feel in your conscience that you have given ground for this treatment, you need not therefore despair; for it is a dear and good token that you have received Christ in repentance. Remember, also, that if you would do any thing against them, you could effect nothing; for it is a godly matter for which you suffer, which God will allow no one but Himself to judge or avenge, as He says by the prophet Zaccharius, 2d chap. 8th verse: "Whoever toucheth you toucheth the apple of my eye."

I can well believe that the poor blind-head, Dr. Wolf Stehlin,[1] is master there; but he will be placed under another sentence than he thinks, and, alas, will become con-

---

[1] An otherwise little-known enemy of Luther's views.

scious of it all too soon. Do thus, my dear sisters, and keep your friends to the same; so will God's grace and peace be with you. Amen.

Take my letter in good part.

MARTINUS LUTHER.

Thursday after Vitus's-day,
    1523.

LETTER III.

To a Noble Lady in a Convent.
December 14, 1523.

The occasion for this letter is shown by its contents.

GRACE to you and peace, honourable and dear maiden Hannah. I have received your letter; and, as you desired, I have diligently helped to promote your projected marriage, both through Herr S. von K. and others who might desire advice, that it may be brought to a right and just end. God knows, that as far as in me lies, I would willingly aid any one in much smaller matters, if I were capable of it. I hear—not unwillingly—that you are disposed towards the married state. But I cannot conscientiously decide on such matters, being absent. For as it concerns more than one person, God has forbidden us to judge on the solicitation of one party; and herein, like yourself, I regard neither noble nor plebeian. One man is as worthy as another, if they have only mutual inclination and love, so that the Evil One may not deceive them.

Have no doubt, therefore, should it happen that I am near, or am asked concerning it, that I will say the best for it, and every where help to promote what is right and just. For as I discover that you have a desire for it, if no injury should occur to any one else by it, it shall be on my part unopposed and unhindered. Only see that you seek God's blessing, and that you are moved not alone by idle worldly love, but by his grace and favour; for I wish you to be united with your dear lover in His grace. Amen.

MARTINUS LUTHER.

Wittenberg,
Monday after Lucia, 1523.

LETTER IV.

To some Nuns.   August 6, 1524.

Advice as to leaving the Convent.

To the Independent Nuns, my dear Sisters in Christ, a friendly letter.

GRACE to you, and peace in Christ Jesus our Saviour. I have from time to time received your letters, and entered into your troubles, and would long ago have given an answer, if I had been moved thereto, and had a messenger been at hand; but I had in other ways much to do. First, have you rightly understood that there are two grounds for abandoning convent life and vows? one is, where the regulations of men and convent work are compulsory, and not voluntary, and the conscience is thereby burdened; this is the time when one should escape, and leave the convent, and let all things go. If, therefore, it is the case with you that the convent work is not of your own free will, but a burden to your conscience, then call upon your friends to help you out and, if the authorities will allow it, provide for you in their homes or elsewhere. If your friends or parents will not consent, let any other good people help you, without regard to whether your parents should be made angry thereby,—should die, or recover from it. For God's will and the salvation of the soul should be before all things, as Christ says : " He who loveth father or mother more than Me, is not worthy of Me." But if the sisters were willing to leave you free, or, at least, to allow you to read or hear the Word of God, you must remain, and do and perform the convent duties, such as spinning, cooking, and the like, provided that you set no value on it. The other ground is the desires of the flesh, however you women-folk are ashamed to acknowledge this ; yet it is to be found in Scripture and experience. As, for instance, eating, drinking, waking, and sleeping are appointed by God, so does He will also that naturally man and woman shall live together in matrimony; therefore is this sufficient, and no one need be ashamed of it, as God has created and made him to this end; so that where there is not high and rare grace, he may go forth and do that for which he is adapted by nature. All these things you will abundantly and sufficiently read and learn, if you come out and hear good sermons. For I have fully proved and set forth these things in the book on Cloister Vows;[1] item, on Eschewing the Teaching of Men;[2] item, in a Sermon on Married Life;[3] item, in the *Postilla*,[4] which, if you read, you will find sufficient instructions in all points, whether it be confession or other things, which are far too long and unnecessary to write; because I foresee that you will leave the convent, whether you are affected by both or only one of these reasons which you put forth in your complaint. If it should come to pass that the convent should attain to true freedom, then those who have grace and liking

---

[1] Walch, xix. p. 1816.   [2] *Id.* xix. p. 712.
[3] *Id.* x. p. 706.
[4] *Church Postilla,* in xi.-xii. vols., by Walch; *House Postilla,* in xiii. vols.

for it may well enter there, even as now the Council at Berne, in Switzerland, has opened the renowned Convent of Königfeld, and allowed any maidens who choose to enter, remain, or go out freely, giving them back what they brought in. Herewith, God be with you; and pray for me.

MARTINUS LUTHER.

Given at Wittenberg,
on the day of Martyr Sixtus, 1525.

LETTER V.

To Katherine Schützin.   December 17, 1524.

Luther congratulates this friend of the Lutheran teaching, who was of some importance in the history of the Reformation at Strasburg, on her faith, and her marriage to the preacher Matthias Zell.

To the virtuous lady, Katherine Schützin, my dear sister and friend in Christ, at Strasburg.

GRACE and peace in Christ. My love, I give you joy that God has so abundantly given you his grace, that you not only perceive and apprehend his kingdom (which is hidden from so many), but also bestow yourself upon a man to whom you may always give ear, and from whom, daily and unceasingly, you may learn what is good; and I wish you grace and strength to continue grateful for the same till that day when, God willing, we shall all see each other and rejoice.

No more now. Pray to God for me, and

give my greeting to your lord, Herr Matthia Zell. Herewith, God be with you.

MARTINUS LUTHER.

Sunday evening, after Service,
    1524.

LETTER VI.

To Maria Queen of Hungary.
November 1, 1526.

Maria, sister of the Emperor Charles V., lost her husband, King Louis II. of Hungary, fighting against the Turks in the battle of Mohacz. She knew Luther's doctrines, and promoted their diffusion. The Psalms of Comfort which Luther dedicated to her were the 37th, 62d, 94th, and 109th.[1]

To her most august Highness and high-born Lady Frau Maria, born Queen of Spain, &c., Queen of Hungary and Bohemia, my most gracious lady.

GRACE and comfort from God our Father, and the Lord Jesus Christ. Most gracious Lady and Queen, I had undertaken, by the recommendation of some pious people, to dedicate to your Queenly Majesty the accompanying four Psalms, as an exhortation that you should cheerfully and vigorously continue

---

[1] Walch, v. 1.

to advance the Holy Word of God in Hungary, because the good tidings came to me that your Queenly Majesty was inclined toward the Gospel, but that you were much hindered and thwarted by the Godless Bishops, who are powerful in Hungary, and are said to have most of the land there ; so that they have caused some innocent blood to be spilt, and terrible violence done against the truth of God. But now, alas ! affairs have changed, through God's power and providence; the Turks having brought great sorrow and misery on your Queenly Majesty, by slaying your beloved husband, the noble young King Ludwig. I therefore am necessitated to change what I had purposed writing. Now, had the Bishop allowed the Gospel to spread, all the world would have cried out that this great misfortune had come to Hungary on account of the Lutheran heresy, which would have been a blasphemy. To whatever now they choose to give the blame, they may see, as I do, that God has hindered any reason from arising for such blasphemy.

As St. Paul writes to the Romans, that the Holy Scriptures are for our consolation, and to teach us patience, I have on that account proceeded to forward these same Psalms to console your Queenly Majesty—so far as God permits us consolation—in this great and sudden misfortune and misery with which the Almighty God has visited at this time your Queenly Majesty,—not from anger or displeasure, as we may justly hope, but as trial and chastisement; that your Queenly Majesty may learn to trust alone in the true Father, who is in heaven, and comfort yourself with the true Bridegroom, Jesus Christ, who is also our Brother—nay, our flesh and blood; and enjoy yourself with the true friends and true associates, the dear angels, who are around, and take care of us. For although that death is so bitter to your Queenly Majesty (and justly so), making you so early a widow, and robbing you of a dear husband, yet again the Scriptures, especially the Psalms, give much good comfort, and show abundantly the sweet-loving Father and Son, in whom lie concealed certain and eternal life.

And, indeed, whoever can arrive so far as to see and feel the love of the Father towards us, as shown in the Scriptures, can also easily bear all the misfortunes that may happen to him on earth. On the other hand, whoever does not feel this, cannot be truly happy, even though he floated in the midst of all the pleasures and enjoyments of the world. Indeed, no man can experience such great misfortune as God the Father Himself experienced, in that his dearest Child was spit upon, cursed, and put to the most shameful death upon the cross, in return for all his wonders and loving deeds; nevertheless, every one thinks his own misfortune the greatest, and lays it more to heart than the crucifixion of Christ, though He had been crucified ten times over. This is because we are not so strong in patience as God is; therefore smaller crosses cause us more woe than the cross of Christ. But may the Father of mercy and God of all comfort console your Queenly Majesty, in his Son Jesus Christ, by his Holy Spirit, that you may soon forget this misery, or be enabled to bear it manfully. Amen.

Your Queenly Majesty's humble servant,

MARTIN LUTHER.

At Wittenberg,
On the 1st of the winter month, 1526.

LETTER VII.

To Frau Dorothea Jörger.
January 6, 1527.

Cristoph Jörger, a Councillor of the Emperor Maximilian I., dwelling in Upper Austria, an adherent of Luther, had received the Esslinger preacher, Michael Stiefel, sent by him. On his return to Wittenberg, Luther writes this letter.

To the noble and virtuous Frau Dorothea Jörger, widow, at Tollet, my best and true friend in Christ.

GRACE and peace in Christ our Lord. Virtuous lady, I have received Michael Stiefel with pleasure, and especially as you bear such good testimony of him, that he has shown himself so Christian-like towards you, and fruitful in good works, as I had expected of him; and God has not caused my confidence to be put to shame. I, together with my Kate, thank you kindly for your dear and true gift. May God Almighty increase and keep you graciously in his Holy Word, as He has begun, to the end. God will rightly overrule this tyranny to his praise and your salvation. Herewith, God be with you. Amen.

MARTINUS LUTHER.

On the Epiphany, 1527.

LETTER VIII.

To Else von Kanitz.   May 2, 1527.

Invitation to become instructress of girls at Wittenberg.

To the honourable and virtuous maiden Else von Kanitz, now at Eiche, my dear friend in Christ.

GRACE and peace in Christ Jesus. Honourable and virtuous maiden Else, I have written to propose to your dear aunt Hanna von Plausig to send you to me for a time; for I have thought of making use of you, to instruct young girls, and that, in beginning such work, you may be an example to others. You shall be in my house and at my table, so that you may be exempt from dangers and cares; so I pray you not to refuse me. I hear that you are tempted with grievous thoughts by the Evil One. O dear maiden, do not let such things frighten you; for those who suffer from the devil here will not do so hereafter: it is a good sign. Christ also suffered thus, and many holy Prophets and Apostles, as is truly shown in the Psalter. Therefore be comforted, and bear willingly this rod from your Father; He will deliver you from it in his good time. When you come, I will speak to you further thereof. Herewith, God be with you. Amen.

At Wittenberg,
Sunday after Agap., 1527.

LETTER IX.

To Elizabeth, Wife of Agricola.[1]
June 10, 1527.

Letter of consolation.

To the honourable and virtuous Frau Elizabeth Agricola, schoolmistress at Eisleben, my dear friend.

GRACE and peace to my dear Elsa. I had wished to write to you earlier, but Herr Matthes was gone sooner than I expected; and so I thought, that if your Herr Magister had returned home, it would, God willing, fare better with you. But you must not be so faint-hearted and despairing, remembering that Christ is near, and helps you to bear evil; for He has not so forsaken you, as to give you up to your own earthly nature.

---

[1] Johann Agricola was preacher at Eisleben. Luther often called him jestingly "Magister Eisleben." He died general superintendent in the Marches.

Only call upon Him with earnest heart, and you may be assured that He will hear you, because you know that it is his nature to help, strengthen, and comfort all those who desire it of Him.

Be therefore comforted, and think that He Himself has suffered far more for you than you can ever suffer on either your own or his account. We will also pray, and pray earnestly, that God will accept you in his Son Christ, and strengthen you in such weakness of body and soul. Herewith God be with you. Amen. Greet your Magister and all yours on all our accounts.

MARTINUS LUTHER.

Given on Whit-Monday, 1527.

LETTER X.

To Frau Felicitas von Selmenitz.
April 1, 1528.

This lady, widow of a former Captain Wolf von Selmenitz, at Allstädt, who had been murdered at Halle, had accepted the Evangelical doctrines, and received the Lord's Supper in both kinds. In 1527, she came with her son for some time to Wittenberg; but went back to Halle on account of the plague. There the archbishop called upon her either to give up her faith, or to abandon Halle. Of this she complained to Luther, and received the following letter from him.

To the honourable, virtuous Frau Felicitas von Selmenitz, widow at Halle, my dear friend in Christ.

GRACE and peace in Christ our Lord and Saviour. Honourable and virtuous lady, I have learnt your trouble. Christ will be with you, and not abandon you. As, however, you inquire of me whether you should flee or remain, I think you are at liberty to flee with a good conscience, if you have received permission from the authorities; but yet I would rather you should delay a while, till you obtain certain news whether the cardinal will come, that it may not be thought you wish to flee before the time and without reason: yet I leave it all to your good pleasure. God Almighty strengthen you and all the brothers and sisters at Halle, according to his Godly will.

MARTINUS LUTHER.

At Wittenberg,
Wednesday, 1st April 1528.

LETTER XI.

To Margaret N.   December 15, 1528.

Consolation on the death of her husband.

GRACE be to you and peace in Christ. Honourable and virtuous lady, your son N. has informed me of the sorrow and misfortune that has come upon you in the death of your dear lord; therefore I am moved by Christian love to write you this letter of consolation.

First, it should comfort you, that in the severe conflict which your lord has sustained, he has at last and finally conquered and won Christ. Furthermore, that he has departed in his senses, and in Christian acknowledgment of our Lord, which I myself have beyond measure gladly and joyfully heard. For Christ Himself struggled in the Garden, and yet at last conquered, and rose from the dead.

But though your lord wounded himself,

it may be that the devil has power over the limbs, and has thus forcibly moved his hand against his will. For if he had done it wilfully, he would not have returned to himself, and been converted to such an acknowledgment of Christ. How often does the devil break an arm, a neck, a back, and all the limbs! He may have power over the body and the limbs without our will.

Therefore you may and ought to be contented in God, and count yourself amongst those of whom Christ says (Matthew v. 4): "Blessed are they that mourn, for they shall be comforted." All saints should sing the 22d verse of the 44th Psalm: "For thy sake are we killed all the day long, and are counted as sheep for the slaughter." We must have sorrow and misfortune, if we are to partake of consolation.

Thank God also for this great mercy, that your lord did not remain in conflict and despair, as happens to some, but was by God's grace powerfully rescued, and was at last taken in Christian confession and faith: of whom it is said: "Blessed are they that die in the Lord." And Christ Himself says (John xi. 26), " He that believeth in Me, though he were dead, yet shall he live." Herewith, may God the Father console and strengthen you in Christ Jesus! Amen.

MARTINUS LUTHER.

At Wittenberg,
Tuesday, Lucia, 1528.

LETTER XII.

To Frau Goritzin. May 5, 1529.

Request to the wife of a judge at Leipzig to be sponsor in Baptism of Luther's daughter, called Magdalene.

GRACE to you, and peace in Christ, honourable and virtuous lady. Dear friend, God having granted that a young heathen should be born to me and my dear Kate, I pray you for God's sake to do us the kindness to help this same poor heathen to become a Christian, and to be her spiritual mother, that she may, by your service and help, throw off the old birth in Adam, and obtain to the new birth in Christ, through holy Baptism. Be assured that I will return your good offices as you may desire. Herewith, God be with you. Amen. I myself have not ventured to go out into the air.

MARTINUS LUTHER.

1529.

LETTER XIII.

To his Wife.   October 4, 1529.

Luther informs her of the result of the Marburger conference, which had been brought about by the Landgrave Philip of Hesse, in order to unite the Swiss Reformers with the Wittenbergers.

GRACE to you, and peace in Christ. Herr Kate,[1] know that our friendly conference at Marburg has come to an end, and we are on almost all points united, except that our opponents maintain that it is mere bread in the Lord's Supper, but acknowledge the presence of Christ therein spiritually. Now the Landgrave is trying to bring us to unanimity, or, in case we continue to disagree, to bind us together as brothers and members of Christ. To this effect he is working eagerly; but we care naught for brothers and members; all we

---

[1] A name frequently applied in jest by Luther to Katherine.

wish is peace and good-will. I think that to-morrow, or the day after, we shall break up, and go to an honourable gentleman at Schl, in Voigtland, whither his Electoral Princely Grace has called us.

Tell Herr Pommer[1] that the best arguments were those of Zwinglius,[2] that "corpus non potest esse sine loco; ergo Christi corpus non est in pane;"[3] and those of Oeckolampadius:[4] the "Sacramentum est signum corporis Christi."[5] I thought that God had blinded them, so that they would advance nothing. I have much to do, and the mes-

---

[1] Johann Bugenhagen, of Pomerania,—on that account generally called by Luther Pommer,—a trusty assistant of Luther. He was professor at Wittenberg, and then general superintendent in Electoral Saxony. He died at Wittenberg, 1558.

[2] Huldreich Zwinglius—born 1484; first Reformer at Zurich—was killed at the battle of Cappel, 1531.

[3] "The body cannot be without place; therefore the body of Christ is not in the bread."

[4] Oeckolampadius (Hausschein), born 1482; pastor and professor at Basle. Died 1531, seven weeks after Zwinglius.

[5] "The Sacrament is the token of the body of Christ."

senger is in a hurry. Say good night to all, and pray for us. We are all fresh and sound, and live like princes. Kiss Lensgen and Hänsgen[1] for me.

Your devoted servant,
MARTINUS LUTHER.

The day of Franciscus, 1529.

P.S. Johann Brenz,[2] Andreas Osian-

---

[1] These two children were born—Magdalene 1529, and Hans 1526. Magdalene died 1542; Hans, as Chancery Counsellor at Königsberg, 1575. In Luther's *Table-Talk* we are told how he behaved during the illness and death of Magdalene. When she was lying very sick, he said to her, "Magdalene, my little daughter, thou wouldest willingly remain with the father here, yet gladly goest to the Father yonder?" She answered: "Yes, dear father, as God wills it." As she was dying, he fell on his knees by the bed, weeping bitterly, and praying that God would redeem her. She then passed away in her father's arms. When she lay in the coffin, he said, "It is a wonderful thing, though feeling assured of all being well with her, and that she is at peace, one should yet feel so sorrowful."

[2] Johann Brenz, born 1499; Reformer in Halle, in Swabia; died 1570.

der,[1] Dr. Stephan,[2] from Augsburg, are come here.

Every one here has become mad with fear of the "sweating sickness."[3] Yesterday fifty were taken ill of it, of whom one or two have died.

---

[1] Andreas Osiander, born 1498; preacher at Nuremberg. Died, as professor at Königsberg, 1552.

[2] Stephan Agricola, confessor to the Empress Anna, then Evangelical preacher at Nuremberg and Eisleben. Died 1547.

[3] An epidemic that was known under the name of the "English sweating sickness."

LETTER XIV.

To Katherine Hornung.   February 1, 1530.

Wolf Hornung had been banished by the Elector Joachim of Brandenburg. The long separation from his wife had occasioned money disputes between them. These Luther sought to compose.

To the Honourable Lady, Katherine Hornung, at Cöllen on the Spree.

GRACE and peace in Christ, honourable and dear lady. You may rest assured that what I now write to you is at the request and desire of your husband, Wolf Hornung. Your conscience may truly tell you, that you cannot be safe under the knavish and worthless contract which was given to you, and extorted from Wolf Hornung (as he says); nor can you, on account of it, claim the protection of your sovereign, nor use it, as it is clearly against the Word of God to interfere in disputes betwixt husband and wife. Therefore, the master who arranged this contract for you, and did not scruple at such a trick, absented himself, and has wished to draw his head out of the noose, and to shove the whole affair off upon Hornung ; but does not see that he has fallen into the trap himself.

Now, you know, you have committed such great and horrible wickedness and offence against your husband, and carried on such robbery, withholding from him yourself and child, and depriving him of house and home, his property and his honour, besides having driven him into misery ; so that he is exposed, like a poor beggar, to great want and poverty ; added to which, he has for more than four years, as a young man, run the risk of danger to his soul : which sins will all fall upon your own head and neck, and will oppress you ; besides which, you have often been called upon, entreated, and prayed, yet have not come. Therefore it is necessary that the matter should be treated in another way. It is right that you should know that I think Wolf Hornung may loose himself from you as from a public adulteress, if you do not comport yourself otherwise, that he may be enabled to begin a fresh life, wherein he may remain, and not pass his time wandering in perpetual exile.

Therefore I fix a time within which you may bethink you how you ought to act, namely, the approaching mid-Lent, that is, Lätare Sunday; meanwhile, you may act as you choose. After Lätare, you shall (God willing) have another small letter to read. Is the poor Wolf Hornung to suffer such robbery? Well, God, who has more than He can ever bestow, will give him another wife, child, house, and home, possessions and honour. With this knowledge, you may decide for yourself. God deliver you from your sins, and bring you to a right feeling! Amen.

Given at Wittenberg,
  February 1, 1530.

LETTER XV.

To the Wife of J. Jonas.[1]   *April* 24, 1530.

GRACE to you, and peace in Christ. Dear Frau, Doctor, and Godmother, I have read your letter to Herr Doctor Jonas, and am well pleased that God has given you a cheerful spirit and good hope, both with respect to the prospect of having a child, and to the damage done to your house. Your lord is not so light of heart, but is very anxious concerning you; and is angry, and scolds and curses lustily about the pulling down of the house, and bears with great impatience living as near the planks as, on account of the space, he is obliged to live. But be comforted; you shall have no trouble about the house, as the affair has been arranged. I hope, also, that God will graciously help you through your time of trouble, and give you

---

[1] Justus Jonas, born 1493, pastor at Halle; afterwards superintendent at Erfurt, where he died, 1555.

twins: but I think it will be a little daughter. These are such strange creatures, and struggle so, that a large house is too small for them; even as the mothers also do, who make the world too narrow for a poor man. Give my greetings to your dear Jost and grandmother, and accept them yourself. Herewith, God be with you. Amen.

MARTINUS LUTHER.

*Given at Coburg,
on St. George's-day,* 1530.

LETTER XVI.

To his Wife.   August 14, 1530.

A short account of the Diet at Augsburg, and of Luther's health.

GRACE to you, and peace in Christ. My dear Kate, this messenger is in such haste to depart, that I have no time to write any thing, but do not like to let him go without a few lines from me. You may tell Herr Johann Pommer, and all, that I will soon write more. We have as yet no news from Augsburg, but expect every hour a letter. We have flying reports that the answer of our opponents will be publicly read; but they would not give any copy to our party, that they might answer it. I do not know whether this is true. Where the light is thus shunned, our friends will not long remain. Since Lorenzo-day I have been almost well, and felt no swimming in my head, which has made me quite brisk in writing. I had before been much plagued by this dizziness. Greet all for me: more another time. God be with you. Amen. Pray hopefully, for the work is well begun, and God will help.

MARTINUS LUTHER.

*Given on Sunday after
   Lorenzo-day*, 1530.

LETTER XVII.

To his Wife. August 15, 1530.

To be delivered into the hands of my dear Herr Frau Katherine Luther.

GRACE to you, and peace in Christ. My dear Kate, just as I had fastened up my letter, I received these from Augsburg; so I detained the messenger, that he might take them with him. From them you will find that our concerns at Augsburg prosper, pretty much as I have said in other letters. Let Peter Weller[1] read them to you, or Herr Johann Pommer. May God continue to help, as He has graciously begun. Amen. I cannot write more now, as the messenger sits ready to depart, and will scarcely tarry. Greet our dear Sack. I have read your

[1] Weller, probably a brother of Jerome Weller, who is mentioned in the 20th Letter, an intimate friend of Luther. Jerome died 1572, as superintendent at Freiberg.

letter to the Treasurer's wife, and she thanks you much. I have sent Hans Polner[1] to Peter Weller: see that he comports himself obediently. Greet Hans Luther, and his schoolmaster, to whom I will soon write. Greet cousin Lehnen,[2] and all the rest. We are eating here ripe grapes, although it has been very wet this month. God be with you all. Amen.

MARTINUS LUTHER.

Ex Eremo,[3] *Assumption-day*, 1530.

P.S. It vexes me that our printer has so shamefully delayed the copies. I send these copies that they may be finished speedily, and they make winter fruit of them for me. If I had wished them to be laid aside, I should have kept them with me. I have written to you to take the sermon[4]

---

[1] A student recommended by Luther.
[2] A relation dwelling in Luther's house.
[3] From the wilderness. Thus Luther called his residence at Koburg.
[4] On the duty of sending children to school.

from Schirlenz (if he has not begun it), and give it to George Ran.[1] I can imagine that Schirlenz has not sufficient paper for his large edition. If you have not given it to the other, let it be done soon, and the sermon finished at the earliest.

[1] Two printers.

LETTER XVIII.

To his Wife. September 24, 1530.

To be delivered into the hands of Frau Katherine D. Luther, at Wittenberg.

GRACE to you, and peace in Christ. My dear Kate, I wrote a letter to you yesterday, which I sent, together with one to our gracious lord, from which you will understand that our people at Augsburg are about to start. Then I hope, God willing, that we shall in a fortnight be with you at home, although I think our affair will not remain uncensured. But they have no power. They positively desire to have the monks and nuns again in the cloisters. Yet Rietesel has written that he hopes that they will part in peace on all sides at Augsburg. May God grant this! it would be a great mercy. It needs that things should go well with us, as the Turks are upon us. You will hear further from Hornung. Herewith, God be with you all. Amen.

MARTINUS LUTHER.

Coburg, Sunday after Matthias, 1530.

LETTER XIX.

To the Wife of Matthew Zell.
January 24, 1531.

This letter has reference to the position of Luther with the Strasburgers.

To the virtuous wife of Matthew Zell, at Strasburg, my kind and dear friend.

GRACE and peace in Christ. My dear lady, I have not hitherto answered your letter which I received long since, as I thought it was too soon whilst the affair was so new; but as now (God be praised!) the bitterness is a little softened, I will enter upon your letter, that you may help to entreat both your lord and other friends, that (if it please God) peace and union may be preserved. For you know full well that love should be above all things, and have the precedence, except of God, who is over all things, and even above love. If He and his Word have the precedence, love will assuredly have the upper hand with us, next to God. Such high things should not be undertaken by our own devices or zeal, but by hearty prayer and spiritual sighs; for it is God's affair, not ours. God must do it; our doing is nothing. Pray, pray, pray; and let Him take care. Herewith, God be with you. Amen. Greet your dear lord for me.

MARTINUS LUTHER.

January 24, 1531.

LETTER XX.

To Barbara Lischnerin.   April 30, 1531.

Luther endeavours to relieve her doubts on predestination.

GRACE to you, and peace in Christ. Dear and virtuous lady, your dear brother Jerome Weller has made known to me how sorely you are troubled with temptation concerning eternal foreknowledge, which is truly grievous to me. May Christ our Lord deliver you from it. Amen.

I know this malady well, and have lain in the hospital on account of it, being sick even to death eternal. Now will I, besides my prayers, give you counsel and comfort. In such matters, writing is a weak thing; but I will not desist, if God will give me grace for it. I will show you how God has helped me out of it, and by what skill I daily maintain myself against it.

First, you must firmly fix in your mind

that such thoughts are assuredly the promptings and fiery darts of the Evil One. The Holy Scriptures speak thus: "He who inquires into the Majesty of the Most High will be cast down." Now, such thoughts are idle searchings into the Majesty of God, and would pry into his high Providence; and Jesus the son of Sirach says, iii. 22: "Thou shalt not inquire into what is too high for thee." But what God has commanded, that do thou accept; for it profits you nothing to gape after that which you are not commanded. David also pleads with the Lord, in Psalm cxxxi. 2, as though it would have fared ill with him, if he had exercised himself in great matters which were too high for him.

Therefore, it is certain that these ideas come not from God, but from the devil, who plagues the heart therewith, that man may hate God, and despair; all which God has strictly forbidden in the first commandment, and wills that we should love, trust, and praise Him by whom we live.

Secondly: if such ideas beset you, you

should learn to ask yourself : " Is it any where commanded, so that I should think of or act upon it ?" If there is no such commandment, learn to say : "Avaunt, thou miserable devil ! thou wishest to drive me to take care of myself, though God every where tells me that I should leave it to Him to take care of me, and says, ' I am thy God !'—that is, ' I care for you'—" hold to Me therefore, and await my bidding, and let Me take care of you." As St. Peter teaches (1 Peter v. 7) : " Cast all your care upon Him, for He careth for you ;" and David (in Psalm lv. 22) : " Cast thy burden upon the Lord, and He shall sustain thee."

Thirdly : if, nevertheless, these thoughts will not leave you (for the devil unwillingly desists), you must also not desist, but always turn your mind from them, and say : " Dost thou not hear, devil, that I will not have such thoughts ? God has forbidden them. Avaunt thee ! I must now think on his commandments, and let Him the while care for me. If thou art so clever in such matters, betake thee to heaven, and dispute with God Himself, who can sufficiently answer thee." Thus will you always drive him from you, and turn your heart to God's commandments.

Fourthly: of all God's commandments, the highest is, that we shall take after the pattern of his dear Son, our Lord Jesus Christ, who should be our daily and most excellent mirror, wherein we see what great love God hath for us; and how highly, in his infinite goodness, He has cared for us, in that He has given his dear Son for us.

In this way, I say, one learns the true knowledge of predestination, and no otherwise; thus will it be shown that you believe in Christ. If you believe, you are called; if you are called, you are also assuredly predestinated. Do not let this mirror and throne of grace ever be torn from the eyes of your heart; but if such thoughts come and bite like fiery serpents, do not give heed to these thoughts or serpents, but ever turn away your thoughts, and contemplate the brazen serpent, that is, Christ given for us; so, God willing, it shall fare better with you.

But, as I have said, you will have to

struggle, and ever shun such thoughts. If they find entrance, cast them out again as you would speedily spit out any filth that had fallen into your mouth. Thus has God helped me; for it is his urgent command that we conform ourselves to his Son, in whom He has abundantly shown Himself to be our God (as the first commandment teaches), who helps and cares for us. Therefore He will not suffer that we should help or take care for ourselves: for that is to deny God, and the first commandment, and Christ.

The miserable devil, who is the enemy of God and Christ, will drag us by such thoughts, contrary to the first commandment, from God and Christ, to rest on ourselves and our own care, that so we may take upon ourselves God's office, which is to care for us and be our God; just as he desired to make Adam in Paradise equal with God, that Adam might be his own God, and take care of himself, and thus rob God of this care and godly work, whereby Adam did so grievously fall.

Thus much have I now advised you, and

have desired your brother Jerome Weller to warn and admonish you with all diligence, that you may cast away such thoughts, and send them home to the devil, that he may fathom them; who knows well how it fared with him before in a like case—namely, that he fell from heaven into the abyss of hell. In short, what is not commanded us should not distract nor trouble us; it is of the devil, not God. May our dear Lord Jesus Christ show unto you his wounds, and gladden your heart with his love, so that you may see and hear Him alone, until you become one with Him in joy! Amen.

D. MARTINUS LUTHER.

The last day of April 1531.

LETTER XXI.

To his Mother. May 20, 1531.

GRACE to you, and peace in Christ Jesus our Lord and Saviour. Amen. My beloved mother, I have received my brother Jacob's letter, with an account of your sickness ; and it grieves my heart, especially as I cannot be with you in person, as I would gladly be ; yet will I be, as it were, in person with you in this letter, together with all our family, and will assuredly not be away from you in spirit.

Although I hope, that not only has your heart been long and abundantly instructed, and (God be praised !) perfected in his comforting Word, but also that you have been provided with preachers and comforters, yet will I do my part, and, as in duty bound, show that I am your child, and recognise you as my mother ; as God our Creator has made and bound us to one another by mutual duties, so that I may add myself to the number of your comforters.

First, dear mother, you know well God's mercy, and how that this your sickness is his gracious fatherly chastisement, and quite a slight one in comparison of that which He inflicts upon the godless, or even upon his own dear children, as one is beheaded, another burnt, and a third drowned, and so forth; and we must all declare: "For thy sake are we killed all the day long; we are counted as sheep for the slaughter" (Ps. xliv. 22; Rom. viii. 36). Therefore this sickness should not afflict nor trouble you, but should be accepted with thankfulness, as sent of his mercy; seeing how slight a suffering it is, even though it should be a sickness unto death, compared with the sufferings of his own dear Son, our Lord Jesus Christ, which He did not suffer for Himself, as we do, who must suffer for our own sins.

Secondly, you know, dear mother, the true main point and foundation of our salvation, whereon should be placed our confidence in this and all troubles; namely, the cornerstone Jesus Christ (Is. xxviii. 16; Rom. ix. 33; 1 Peter ii. 6), who will not waver nor fail us, nor allow us to sink and perish. For He is the Saviour, and calls Himself the Saviour of all poor sinners (1 Tim. ii. 4), and of all who are in tribulation and about to die, who have relied on Him, and called on his Name.

He saith: "Be of good cheer; I have overcome the world." If He has overcome the world, He has assuredly overcome the prince of this world, with all his power. And what is his power but death, whereby He has prostrated us and made us prisoners on account of our sins? But now that death and sin are overcome, may we joyfully and cheerfully hear the sweet words: "Be of good cheer; I have overcome the world"!

And we must not doubt their truth; but, as we are commanded, accept them with joy and comfort and thanksgiving. And he who will not be comforted by these words does the greatest injustice and dishonour to the dear Comforter, just as if it were not true when He bids us be of good cheer; or as if it were not true that He has overcome the world: and thus we ourselves restore the tyranny of the vanquished devil, sin, and death, against the dear Saviour—from which God preserve us!

Therefore let us now rejoice in all security and gladness; and should any thought of sin or death arise to frighten us, let us raise our hearts, and say, "Behold, dear soul, what doest thou? Dear death, dear sin, why dost thou live and frighten me? Seest thou not that thou art conquered? and that thou, death, art dead? Knowest thou not One who has said of thee, 'I have overcome the world'? It becometh not me to listen or give heed to thy terrors, but only to the cheering words of my Saviour: 'Be comforted, be of good cheer; I have overcome the world.' He is the Conqueror, the true Hero, who hereby gives and appropriates his victory to me. Be of good cheer. On Him I rest, to his words and comfort I cling; thereby I remain here, or journey thither: He will not deny me. By thy false terrors thou wouldst gladly deceive me, and with lying thoughts would rend me from such a Conqueror and Saviour; and they are as surely lies, as it is true that He has overcome, and commanded us to be comforted. Thus, St. Paul also boasts and defies the terrors of death (1 Cor. xv. 54, 55): 'Death is swallowed up in victory. O death, where is thy sting? O grave, where is thy victory?' Frighten and irritate thou canst, like a wooden image of death; but thou hast no power to destroy. For thy victory, sting, and power have been swallowed up in Christ's victory; thou mayest show thy teeth, but thou canst not bite. For God has given us the victory through Christ Jesus our Lord, to whom be praise and thanks. Amen."

With such words and thoughts, and none other, dear mother, you may set your heart at rest, and be thankful that God has brought you to such knowledge, and not allowed you to stick in the errors of Popery, by which we are taught, to rely on our own works and the holiness of monks, and to consider this our only Comforter and Saviour, not as a comforter, but as a severe judge and tyrant,—to flee from Him to Mary and the saints, and not to expect of Him any mercy or comfort.

But now we know far otherwise of the unfathomable compassion and goodness of our Heavenly Father, and that Jesus Christ is our Mediator (1 Tim. ii. 5) and stepping-stool of grace, and our Bishop in heaven before God, who daily intercedes for us, and atones for all (Rom. iii. 25) who only call upon and believe in Him (Heb. iv. 16; vii. 25); and is not a severe judge, except to those who do not believe in Him, nor accept his comfort and grace. He is not one who accuses and threatens us, but who intercedes and atones by his own death, having shed his blood for us; so that we ought not to fear Him, but approach Him with all assurance, and call Him dear Saviour, sweet Comforter, true Bishop of our souls (1 Tim. iv. 10; 1 Pet. ii. 25).

To such knowledge, I say, God has graciously called you, whose sign and seal you have—namely, the Gospel, Baptism, and the Sacrament; you also hear preaching, so that you shall have no danger nor trouble. Only be comforted, and joyfully thankful for such great mercy; for He who has begun will also graciously perfect it in you. But we cannot help ourselves in such matters—we can gain nothing over sin, death, and the devil by our own works; therefore there is One for us in our stead, who can do better, and give to us his victory, so that we accept and do not doubt thereof; and He says: "Be of good cheer; I have overcome the world;" and again: "Because I live, ye shall live also; and your joy no man taketh from you" (John xvi. 22; xiv. 19).

The Father and God of all comfort grant you, through his holy Word and Spirit, a firm, joyful, and thankful faith, whereby you may overcome this and all other trouble, and at last feel and experience that it is the truth when He Himself says: "Be of good cheer; I have overcome the world." I herewith commend your body and soul to his mercy. Amen. All your children and my Kate pray for you. Some weep, others eat, and say grandmother is very ill. God's grace be with us all! Amen.—Your dear son,

MARTINUS LUTHER.

Sunday evening after Ascension Sunday, 1531.

LETTER XXII.

To his Wife. February 27, 1532.

Luther, being at Court on account of the illness of the Elector, writes from thence this letter.

To be delivered into the hands of my dearly beloved wife, Katherine Luther.

GOD greet you in Christ, my beloved Kate. I trust, if Doctor Brüch[1] permits, as he gives me hope he will, that I shall be with you tomorrow or the next day. God grant that He may bring us home fresh and sound. I sleep exceeding well about six or seven hours together, and then one or two hours afterwards. It is owing to the beer, I think; but I am temperate, as at Wittenberg. Doctor Caspar[2] says that the canker in the foot of our most gracious lord does not spread fur-

---

[1] Gregory Brüch was Chancellor to the Elector.
[2] Professor of Theology and Court Preacher at Wittenberg.

ther; but no Dobitzch,[1] nor prisoner on the ladder in the prison of Hans the gaoler, ever suffered such martyrdom as his Electoral Grace suffers from the surgeons. His Princely Grace is as sound all over as a roach; but the devil has bitten and stung his foot. Pray, pray yet more. I hope that God will hear us, as He has already done; for Dr. Caspar considers that none but God can help here. As Johannes[2] will go away, it is necessary,

---

[1] Probably the name of some malefactor.

[2] On the same day, Luther wrote the following letter of recommendation for this servant:

"I, D. Martinus Luther, preacher at Wittenberg, beg, for Christ's sake, of all who love God's Word, that they will favourably recommend the bearer of this letter, Johannes Nischmann, who has faithfully, industriously, and humbly served me for some years, and that they will assist him to the utmost, on account of the Lord, for whose sake he has served me. As truly as our Gospel and Christ Himself are true, will this be, without doubt, a pleasing and acceptable service to God. And when I can return these good offices, I shall be always willing and ready to do so. Herewith, God be with you.

"MY OWN HAND.

"*Tuesday after Reminiscere*, 1532."

and honour demands, that I should let him depart in honour. For you know that he has faithfully and industriously served us, and demeaned himself humbly according to the Gospel, and done and borne all things. Be mindful how oft we have given to good-for-nothings and thankless scholars, on whom it has been thrown away; therefore be liberal, and do not let such a pious fellow want, as you know that it is important, and pleasing to God. I know well that there is little in hand; but I would gladly give him ten gulden if I had them. But you should not give him less than five gulden, as he has no clothes. Give what more you can, I beg of you. There might, indeed, be given, out of consideration for me, somewhat out of the common chest to such a servant, seeing that I must keep my servants at my own cost for the service and use of the Church; but let them do as they please. Do not stint while there is a cup remaining. Think where you have gained it all. God will certainly give something else—that I know. Herewith, God be with you. Amen.

Ask the pastor of Zwickau[1] to make shift and be satisfied with the lodgings. When I come, I will relate to you how Mühlfurt[2] and I were guests with Riedtesel,[3] and Mühlfurt exhibited to me much knowledge; but I was not in a mood for such drink. Fondle young Hansen for me, and desire Hänschen, Lehnchen, and cousin Lehnen to pray for me and the dear Prince. I cannot find any thing in this town, although the fair is now going on, to buy for the children. If I bring nothing especial, you must get me somewhat.

D. MARTINUS LUTHER.

Tuesday after Reminisc., 1532.

[1] Nicholas Haussmann, one of Luther's truest friends.
[2] Burgermaster at Zwickau.
[3] Electoral Treasurer, and godfather to Luther.

LETTER XXIII.

To Frau Dorothea Jörger. March 7, 1532.

Answer to an offer of assistance to poor students.

To the noble, virtuous Lady Dorothea Jörger, widow, at Tollet, my kind lady, and good friend in Christ.

GRACE and peace in Christ. Noble, virtuous lady, I have received your letter to me, together with the *quince jam*, as has also my dear Kate hers, with the four Hungarian gulden; and we both thank you most kindly. I have also sent Herr Michel Stiefel his, and expect the answer every hour. As you inquire in your letter how I think the five hundred gulden you purpose for poor students of the Holy Scriptures may best be applied, I have, together with *Magistro Philippo*,[1] and other good gentlemen and friends, considered it best, as it is to be ap-

---

[1] Melancthon.

plied to such a necessary and useful work, that it should be put out at interest, that it may be made useful for all time, and for many. For one can render good aid by means of such interest to two persons yearly, if the money is well invested; and we will commend it to the control of the University of Wittenberg. Afterwards, I took pains to write to Lazarus Spengler,[1] Syndic at Nuremberg, that he should inquire at Linz, through trusty agents (as he knows well how to do), for these gulden, and take them in virtue of your handwriting, which I sent him with mine (to be returned), begging him at the same time to exert himself that they may be booked and registered at the Town-hall at Nuremberg, which would be the most secure; if not, to send them to me, that they might be otherwise put out. If this opinion pleases you, the affair will be all straight. I will, for my own part, do the best I can, and rejoice that God has moved your heart to bethink you of such a good work in Christ. For, alas! now among us, though God's Word

---

[1] A faithful adherent of Luther.

be abundantly preached, almost to weariness, of such grace there appears little or next to nothing, but rather the reverse; so that they leave their poor pastors almost to starve. Whether it be nobles, peasants, or citizens, every one is more inclined to rob than to help. But perhaps it is according to the proverb: "The nearer Rome, the worse Christian." And as Christ says in Matthew xii. 42: "The queen of the south shall rise up in the judgment with this generation, and shall condemn it: for she came from the uttermost parts of the earth," &c. To the same dear Lord Jesus Christ I commend you, together with all yours, and to his abundant grace. Amen.

D. MARTINUS LUTHER.

Thursday after Oculi, 1532.

LETTER XXIV.

To Frau von Stockhausen.
November 27, 1532.

Luther gives her advice concerning the depression of her husband.

To the honourable and virtuous Frau N. von Stockhausen, wife of the Captain at Nordhusen, my kind and good friend.

GRACE and peace in Christ. Honourable and virtuous lady, I have written in haste a consolatory note to your dear lord. Now the devil hates you both, because you love Christ, his enemy. For this He must compensate you, as He Himself says: "Because I have chosen you, therefore the world (and its prince) hateth you: but be of good cheer." The sufferings of his saints are precious in the sight of God. As I am in haste, I can write little. Be careful not to leave your husband one moment alone, nor any thing with him whereby he might injure himself. Solitude is poison to him; therefore the devil drives him to it. If you read, or tell him histories, news, and remarkable events, there is no harm,—even though there were sometimes idle or false tittle-tattle, and tales of Turks, Tartars, and the like,—if he be excited thereby to laugh and joke; and then, speedily afterwards, cheering sentences from the Holy Scriptures. Whatever you do, leave him not alone, nor let there be silence around him, that he may not sink into thought. It does not signify if he is angry about it. Act as if it were disagreeable to you, and pretend to scold; but let it be done all the more. This must content you,—in much haste. Christ, who causes you such sorrow of heart, will help you, as He has lately done. Only hold fast to Him. You are the apple of his eye; whosoever touches it, touches Himself. Amen.

DOCTOR MARTINUS LUTHER.

*At Wittenberg, Wednesday after
    St. Catherine, 1532.*

LETTER XXV.

To Frau Jörger.   *May* 6, 1533.

On the subject of Letter XXIII.

GRACE and peace to you. Honourable and virtuous lady, your letter concerning the five hundred gulden, which ought to have been received at Linz last Easter, came to me too late. I have, nevertheless, according to your request, begged of and admonished Martin Seldener, through Herr Lazarus Spengler, that he would obtain a bill of exchange, such as is customary, and send it to Nuremberg. However, I should have preferred, as I had before written, that you should yourself have forwarded it in the safest way you could; having also observed from your letter, that you would be better pleased to give this alms out of hand to poor students than to put it to interest ; if you remain of this opinion, I will not dissent.

You must not vex yourself, nor be disturbed, because a preacher has given you anxiety, on account of your son and of the judge, as Herr Michel has informed me. Let them go to law with one another; the affair does not personally concern you: the law will soon settle the business, and your conscience need not be troubled about it.[1] God be with you, and your dear children, and all yours. Amen.

Your devoted
D. MARTINUS LUTHER
(STILL AILING).

Datum Wittenberg,
 May 6, 1533.

[1] Nothing more is known of this family concern.

LETTER XXVI.

To Frau Jörger. October 24, 1532.

On the subject of Letters XXIII. XXV.

GRACE to you, and peace in Christ. Noble and virtuous lady, I have to inform you that the five hundred gulden, in good solid coin, on your account, have arrived, through Wolfgang Seldener, at Leipzig, and have been forwarded by George Kirmeyer from thence to Wittenberg; and I will dispense them according to your request and desire, not forgetting Herr Andres. And I have already, with the advice of certain good friends and gentlemen, decided on the disposal of one hundred. But the same good gentlemen and friends have suggested, that if the other four hundred were put out to interest, and thus two exhibitions founded, two students would be assisted every three years. But I answered that, according to your letter, it was your will that they should be distributed at once. They begged of me, however, to write, and ask you whether it was still your determination to distribute this money forthwith among these poor fellows who study the Holy Scriptures, or whether it might be used for the foundation of two perpetual studentships,—which they consider would be for the best. According to their request, I therefore now write to you, and beg that you will once more write to me what you wish and think best, and I will faithfully execute it. Meanwhile, in order that I may not show disrespect to the request of these good gentlemen, the four hundred gulden shall remain in hand till I obtain your answer. Herewith, may God preserve you and all yours, and may He be well pleased with your faithful work to his praise and honour! Amen.

Michel[1] has experienced a small trial; but it will not injure him—rather, God be praised, profit him.

D. MARTINUS LUTHER.

October 24, 1533.

[1] Michel Stiefel had prophesied the near approach of the last day, and was in much trouble concerning it.

RECEIPT.

I, Martin Luther, D. and Preacher at Wittenberg, acknowledge by this my handwriting that 500 fl., in good solid coin, have been delivered to me here at Wittenberg in my little study, on behalf of the noble and virtuous Frau Dorothy Jörger, widow: to be distributed among poor fellows who study the Holy Scriptures, as she has begged me to do by letter. This money has been delivered to me through George Fonwibler, citizen of Leipzig, agent of Andreas Kirmeyer, of Nuremberg. Done the 24th October 1530. Signed and sealed with my usual signet.

LETTER XXVII.

To the Abbess of Hervord, in Westphalia. Written together with Melancthon. January 15, 1534.

Answer to the complaints of the Princess Abbess of encroachments on her rights.

To the honourable, high-born Lady, Anna Fraulein von Limpurg, Abbess of the chartered, noble Convent at Hervord, our gracious lady.

GRACE and peace through our Lord Jesus Christ. Honourable and high-born lady, since your Grace complains that certain persons at Hervord attempt to encroach upon your Grace's jurisdiction, and to obtain forcibly money and other privileges, know that I, Doctor Martinus, have always written and taught most diligently that the distinction of authority should be upheld, and that no one should seek to rule in another's jurisdiction, nor take or withdraw the revenue of others, or the like. Therefore the said proceedings, concerning which your Grace writes, we disapprove; and heartily wish that those who would thus violently act should bethink them that such conduct dishonours the holy Gospel, and causes it to be hated, which justly grieves every pious Christian. We have, therefore, written to Doctor Johann Dreger, and admonished and begged of him not to participate in such violence and injustice, but to censure such as would practise it, and exhort them to Christian love, which he, as preacher, is bound to do. But the desire of your Grace, that we should write to the Council, we have considered not likely to be profitable, although we do not know exactly what the Church regulations at Hervord may be. But we beg of your Grace, in what concerns the necessary Church offices, to bear with patience the circumstances of these times, and not to seek your rights too sharply in every thing; because your Grace knows that hitherto in many places the churches have been badly supplied both with parsons and with maintenance for them. If, however, certain fortunate changes should have happened in the exigencies of the Church, we beg that your Grace will nevertheless, for the sake of peace, have patience; but we do not approve that certain persons should, contrary to the will of the authorities, take Church property for building the city walls. May God always preserve your Grace! The 11 fl. sent here by your Grace we return; and are ever ready to serve your Grace.

      MARTINUS LUTHER.
      PHILIPPUS MELANCTHON.

Given at Wittenberg,
Thursday, January 15, 1534.

LETTER XXVIII.

To Frau Jörger.   April 27, 1534.

On the subject of Letter XXVI.

GRACE to you, and peace in Christ. Honourable and virtuous lady, I write to inform you that—God be praised!—your alms have been well laid out, and have given aid to many poor, and do so still; and I cannot doubt that God, who has put it into your heart to do this, will openly show that it is well pleasing to Him as a precious thank-offering, whereby you acknowledge and praise the mercy which He has shown you through his Son Jesus Christ. May God strengthen you in steadfast faith, and happily accomplish the work He has begun in you! Amen. I did not myself know, nor could I have believed, that there were in this small town and poor school so many clever and pious fellows, who have lived on bread and water, and have suffered cold and frost, that they might be able to study God's Word and Scriptures, to whom your alms have been a great comfort and refreshment. I have already dispensed above half, and received testimony that it has been given to upright fellows, not to worthless lads. I have not delayed telling you this, that you might know how your money is being spent. I have given to Andres more than the others: first 10 fl., then again 10 fl., and among the others 2, 3, and 4 fl. each, according to the advice of good friends; and they are all glad and thankful. This little book is sent you as a token, by desire of Michel Stiefel, to whom, as he is without a benefice, I have given 10 fl.; and he greets you heartily. Christ be with you, and all yours. Amen.

MARTINUS LUTHER, D.

Monday after Jubilate, 1534.

LETTER XXIX.

To his Wife. July 29, 1534.

From Court, where he is detained on account of the illness of the Elector.

To my kind and dear master, Frau Katherine von Bora D. Lutherin, at Wittenberg.

GRACE and peace in Christ. Dear Herr Kate, I have nothing to write to you, as M. Philipp and the others are returning home. I must remain here longer, on account of the pious Prince. You may judge how long I am likely to remain here, and bethink you how you may help to release me. I expect that M. Franciscus[1] will relieve me, as I did him, but not so soon. Yesterday I had bad stuff to drink, and was made to sing. It is an annoyance to me to have bad wine to drink, when I remember what good wine and beer I have at home, besides a pretty wife—or, shall I say it, master? You

[1] Franz Burkhard, Electoral Vice-Chancellor.

would do well to send over to me a whole cellar full of my wine, and a bottle of your beer as often as you can; for I shall not return till you have the new beer. Herewith, God be with you and our children, and all the folk. Amen.

    Your beloved,
        MART. LUTHER, D.

Wednesday after Jacobi, 1534.

LETTER XXX.

To an Unknown Person.   March 7, 1535.

Whether the Lord's Supper might be received in both kinds at home.

God's grace to you, and peace in Christ. Honourable and virtuous lady, your dear brother N. has informed me how desirous you are of the holy Sacrament in both kinds, and doubtful whether you may receive them privately in your own house.

Although there has been such a custom in Popedom, and the element has been administered in houses at private mass, yet, for the sake of example, and other reasons, I cannot advise it. For in the course of time every one might so use it, that the general assembly and church would thereby be abandoned and deserted, so that it would no longer be a public and general profession. On the other hand, if it can be done, and you wish for it, and will venture, your conscience approving, then do it, in God's name, to whom I recommend you in my poor prayers.

D. MART. LUTHER.

Given, Dominica Lätare.

LETTER XXXI.

To Frau Jörger. April 3, 1535.

With reference to Letter XXVIII.

GRACE to you, and peace in Christ. Virtuous, honourable, and dear lady, Master Andres has told me that he cannot go to you without a letter from me, explaining that the air of this place does not suit his health, and drives him away: he will tell you all the circumstances. It is as the Scripture says: "Some are hungry; others are full." With you there is a hunger and thirst for the Word of God; with us many are so satiated and weary, that it must grieve God. Well, the world is the world; God help us all. Your alms have, God be praised, helped many good people who study diligently the Holy Scriptures; for many who have been driven from other countries for the Word's sake, and lived among us on bread and water, have been made glad, in that they have been enabled by your alms to buy books, and sometimes clothing. It will be well pleasing to Christ our Lord, who has put it into your heart to do it. I, as Master Andres will tell you, am sometime strong, sometime well, sometime joyful, sometime sad. But Christ is at all times the Lord, and will, shall, can, and must ever remain so. Amen. Master Michel Stiefel has again a benefice, and is now better than before. Christ our dear Lord guard, strengthen, and prepare you and all yours for his blessed future, together with us all. We wish and gladly desire that He may come soon; for the world will every where become wicked. This helps us to pray against this same world.

MARTINUS LUTHER, D.

Thursday after Ambrosius, 1535.

LETTER XXXII.

To the same. September 12, 1535.

GRACE to you, and peace in Christ, with my poor Paternoster, &c. Revered and dear lady, I have heard Master Andres, and received your letter; and I thank you for the gift, especially on account of the little groschen, although I would gladly be sure whether it were a genuine one, because it looks so new; but it may be counterfeit, or a cast. Master Andres has also informed me that you would be glad to know whether, with a good conscience (if the pastor will allow it), you can have the Gospel preached for your own household alone, the other parishioners being excluded. If you have permission from the pastor to have it in the house, you may use it till you are prevented by force; for you are not bound to interfere on behalf of others against the dictates of the authorities. Every one must take his own hazard, and abide his own venture. For the rest, do not be disturbed if the preacher is not anointed and shaven by the bishop; for they are not consecrated to the office of preacher, but for secret mass, and are priests of Baal and Jeroboam. He who is called is consecrated, and should preach to those who call him; that is our Lord God's consecration, and the true anointing oil. My wife greets you and yours kindly. Herewith, God be with you. Amen.

MARTINUS LUTHER, D.

At Wittenberg, Sunday after the birth of our dear Lady, 1535.

LETTER XXXIII.

To the same. July 13, 1536.

She was anxious lest there should arise strife betwixt her sons and daughters, on account of their maternal inheritance. The daughters had resigned it; but the mother wishes them to have an equal share with the sons, who would not agree to it. Luther gives his advice, and begs for the prolongation of maintenance to a person in need.

To the much honoured noble lady, Dorothea Jörger, widow, at Keppach, my kind lady and good friend.

GRACE and peace in Christ. Much-honoured, dear lady, Master Andres Hechel has told me of your wish to make a will for the advantage of your daughters, but that your sons will not consent, because your daughters have beforehand resigned both their paternal and maternal portion; and you ask good counsel thereupon. My opinion is, that if you can further it with your sons by kindness, so that they may consent, it may be accomplished; but if that cannot be, and if your daughters have already resigned their claim, your conscience need not be troubled if you are not able to restore what they have given up. Therefore do not vex yourself therewith.

Besides this, Master Andres has asked me to write and beg of you to extend your bounty to him till Easter, and thus enable him to continue his study this short space of time. Thus you will act kindly and Christianly. Herewith, God be with you, and all yours. My better half, Frau Kate, sends you friendly greeting.

MARTINUS LUTHER, D.

At Wittenberg, Monday after St. Jacobi, 1536.

LETTER XXXIV.

To his Wife.   February 27, 1537.

Luther, from Gotha, informs her of an attack of illness.

GRACE to you, and peace in Christ. Dear Kate, you may for the present hire such horses as you are in need of; for my gracious lord will keep your horses, and send home M. Philipp with them. For I myself yesterday set out from Schmalkalden, and travelled from thence in my gracious lord's own carriage. The reason of this is, that I have not been in good health for three days, and have neither rested nor slept, nor been able to eat or drink. In short, I have been nigh unto death, and did commend you and my children to God and my good lord, as though I should never see you again. I had much pity for you, but had resigned myself to the grave. Now, however, the tears of many people and earnest prayers to God have so worked, that it appears to me I am born again.

Therefore thank God, and let the dear children and cousin Lenen thank the true Father; for you would assuredly have lost this father. The pious Prince has set people running and riding and fetching, and tried to the utmost of his power to aid me; but it was of no avail. Your skill and remedy also have done nothing. God has done wonders for me, and has done it through the intercession of pious people.

I write this to you, for I believe that my gracious lord has ordered the Land Vogt (Governor) to send you to me, lest I should die on the road, that you might ere that see and speak to me; but it is now unnecessary, and you may remain at home, as God has so abundantly aided me, that I look forward to a joyful return to you. To-day we stay at Gotha. I have besides this written to you four times, and wonder much you have received nothing.

MARTINUS LUTHER.

Tuesday after Reminiscere, 1537.

LETTER XXXV.

To an Unknown Person. *May* 24, 1537.

Short letter of consolation.

GRACE and peace to my dear Frau N. I had wished to write to you earlier; but Master N. was gone sooner than I expected, and I thought that if your lord had returned home, it would, God willing, fare better with you. But you must not be so faint-hearted and despairing; but remember that Christ is near, and helps you to bear evil; for He has not so forsaken you as to give you up to your own earthly nature. Only call upon Him with earnest heart, and you may be assured that He will hear you, because you know that it is his nature to help, strengthen, and comfort all those who desire it of Him.

Be therefore comforted, and think that He Himself has suffered far more for you than you can ever suffer on either your own or his account. We will also pray, and pray earnestly, that God will accept you in his Son Christ, and strengthen you in such weakness of body and soul. Herewith, God be with you. Amen.

MARTINUS LUTHER.

On Whit-Monday, 1537.

LETTER XXXVI.

To the Duchess Elizabeth of Brunswick.
September 4, 1538.

Thanks for a present—Sends some cuttings.

GRACE to you, and peace in Christ. Most serene and high-born Princess and gracious Lady, I and my dear Kate thank your Princely Grace for the cheese. This present is the more dear to us, even though it were less, as your Serene Highness, by God's grace, shows such an earnest regard for his Holy Word. And we pray that the Father of all mercy, through his dear Son, may abundantly endow your Princely Grace with his Holy Spirit, and preserve you to the day of eternal redemption. We commend ourselves to your Princely Grace as willing servants. Amen. I send herewith to your Princely Grace plants of mulberry and fig-trees, as many as I have at present. Besides these, I have nothing rare.

Your Princely Grace's devoted,
MARTINUS LUTHER.

Wednesday after Ægidi, 1538.

LETTER XXXVII.

To Ursula Schneidewin, at Stollberg.
June 4, 1539.

To the honourable, virtuous lady Ursula Schneidewin, widow, citizen at Stollberg, my kind, good friend.

GRACE and peace in Christ. Honourable, virtuous, dear Lady, I have written to you concerning your son John, that he has conceived a great love for an honourable maiden here; and as you must have received my opinion, I hoped you might have given a favourable answer; but as the delay appears to me too long, I feel it necessary to urge you further. For I am not unfavourably disposed towards him, and would not that he should be driven to despair. As, therefore, the maiden so greatly pleases him, is not unequal to him in station, and is besides a gentle, good girl, of honourable extraction, it appears to me you may well be contented, as he has humbled himself as a child, and begged for the maiden as did Samson. Therefore it is fitting for you, as a loving mother, to give your consent; for though we have written that children should not betroth themselves without the consent of their parents, we have also written, that parents should not, nor, according to God's will, can control or hinder their children at their own pleasure. No son should bring a daughter to his parents without their consent; but also a father should not force a wife upon his son. They should do their best on both sides, otherwise the son's wife must become the father's daughter without his approval. Who knows what happiness God may provide for your son by means of this maiden, which, perhaps, otherwise may be lost to him, especially as the good maiden gives fair hopes, is not unequal in station, and her sorrow might become a curse? In short, I beg you will no longer delay your assent, that the good fellow may be relieved from his disquiet. For I cannot delay longer; but must take measures on account of my office. But I beg you will not

let this letter be known to your son John;
for he ought not to know it till the matter is
settled, that he may not be too confident and
bold. For I love him, of which he is well
worthy, on account of his goodness, and therefore
would not advise him to his harm. Therefore
do your part as a mother, and relieve him
from this torment, that he may not be obliged
to do it in spite of you. Herewith, God be
with you. Amen.

MARTINUS LUTHER, DR.

Wednesday after Trinity, 1539.

LETTER XXXVIII.

To the same. *July* 10, 1539.

GRACE to you, and peace in Christ. Honourable and virtuous lady, I have, if I am not mistaken, written to you twice concerning your son John, who, as a good son, has begged you, through me, to show yourself a kind mother, as you ought, and give your consent to his marriage with this maiden, thereby doing his duty as a son, as Samson did to his parents. I have also told you that I can no longer delay, but think fit, as I purpose faithfully by him, that he should be delivered from this danger; for I see that his studies are hindered, and that no good can come if you are so harsh with him. What I do is for your honour: she is his equal, the child of good people. Besides, you must bethink you that it is not bearable that the children of other people should be excited to love, and afterwards, without cause, neglected, which you would hardly suffer to be done by your children; therefore it must not be, especially where it is a question of marriage. I have further written and advised that you should not refuse, that we may not be compelled to proceed notwithstanding. I have indeed written that children should not betroth themselves without the consent of their parents; but I have also written, that parents should not hinder their children; and, in short, I cannot now repeat what I have written to you before, and I justly wonder that I have received no answer. It is so annoying to me that my boarder should delude our citizen's daughter, that I again beg you will give a speedy, favourable answer, otherwise we must do what we can to prevent scandal. You have been sufficiently entreated: when parents will not decide, the pastor must. If you are anxious how he is to maintain himself, remember that one must put one's trust in God, who gives his support to the married state; I will never, as long as I live, abandon John: nevertheless, he himself will, God willing, prosper without my help. I therefore beg you will show signs of life; for I am weary of writing so often on a matter in which you have no reason to object, otherwise I must suppose that you behave yourself thus to me on account of your son, which would be annoying to me, as I have always intended kindly by you and yours. Herewith, God be with you. Amen. And a short, right answer from you.

MARTINUS LUTHER, DR.

Thursday after Kiliani, 1539.

LETTER XXXIX.

To the Duchess Katherine of Saxony.
July 28, 1539.

A request concerning the management of the Church visitation in the dominions of Duke Henry, the husband of Katherine.

To the serene, high-born Princess and Lady, Katherine, born Duchess of Mecklenburg, Duchess of Saxony, Landgravine of Thuringia, and Margravine of Meissen, my gracious lady.

GRACE and peace in Christ. Serene, highborn Princess, and gracious Lady; as my gracious lord Duke Henry is old and weak, and the government new, difficult, and over-much for his Princely Grace; and, indeed, Master Antonius[1] alone, with those near him, cannot do all; and as I hope your Princely Grace has less work,—my humble request is, that your Princely Grace would sometimes help to urge on matters, and desire that the visi-

---
[1] Antonius Lauterbach, pastor at Leipzig.

tation may proceed with proper dignity; for there are certain bad people at Leipzig who constantly hope that it may be delayed, and finally fall to ashes. A little book also is about to be put forth against the visitors; if that be so, we must answer it. Here might Y. P. G. help, that a flame may not burst out. They have, perhaps, their abettors, and need stern measures, that they may learn obedience; otherwise, it would appear that they let one order what one will, and they do what they please. May Y. P. G. turn your mind with gracious diligence to honour the Word of God, and to guard against the devil; this will be the most agreeable sacrifice and prayer to God the Father, to whose grace I commend Y. P. G. Amen.

Your Princely Grace's obedient,
MARTINUS LUTHER.

Monday after Jacobi, 1539.

LETTER XL.

To Dorothea, the wife of B. Mackenrot, at Rossla, Luther's Sister. December 2, 1539.

Announcement of his visit at Rossla; but this letter is probably of an earlier period than would appear from its date.

To be delivered to Frau Dorothea, the beloved Wife of Herr Balthazar Mackenrot, attendant on the Prince, at Rossla.

DEAR SISTER,—I have seen, from the letter you sent me, how your deeply troubled conscience longs for the comfort of evangelical preaching, and how you desire that you may some day hear it in your church at Rossla. I have greatly rejoiced thereat; and have now resolved in God, if He grants me health and strength, to be with you certainly on the approaching holy Christmas Eve, and, by God's help, to begin the first evangelical preaching at Rossla and Upper Rossla, and to perform it as a remembrance. Greet your husband and little daughter Margaret, to whom I will bring something; and God be with you.

MARTINUS LUTHER, D.

Given at Eisleben,
  Dec. 2, 1539.

LETTER XLI.

To the Duchess Elizabeth of Brunswick.
January 29, 1540.

Letter of recommendation.

To the most serene, high-born Princess and Lady, Frau Elizabeth, born Margravine of Brandenburg, and Duchess of Brunswick and Lüneburg, my gracious lady.

GRACE and peace in Christ. Most serene, high-born Princess, gracious Lady, the bearer of this, Magister Justus Waldhausen, son of a citizen at Hamel, called to be Recorder there, has begged of me to write to your Princely Grace, as he has now for twelve years been accustomed to our Gospel, which, perhaps, is not in use at Hamel. May Y.P.G. please to be gracious to him, and protect him as much as possible; and also request your princely husband to hold such-like persons in esteem. For, as Y. P. G. will perceive, he is a learned, clever, pious man, such as one does not often find. May Y. P. G. be graciously inclined to him: it will be for the advantage of the people and country, as he can and will be useful. By this, Y. P. G. also will do especial service. Herewith, I commend you to the dear God. Amen.

   Your Princely Grace's obedient,
       MARTINUS LUTHER.

*Thursday after the Conversion
 of St. Paul,* 1540.

LETTER XLII.

To the Duchess Katherine of Saxony.
June 25, 1540.

Luther again recommends to her the cause of the Reformation.

I AGAIN pray of Y. P. G., with all submission, that you will, as you gave me at Leipzig great hopes you would, earnestly and diligently help the churches and schools, that they may not be forgotten nor neglected. This is the highest service you can render to God. For I hear and see much that I should not have expected, and which truly displeases me; not that my displeasure signifies much, unless it be displeasing to God Himself, and cannot come to a good end. God grant Y. P. G. courage, so to see and do (as God has given Y. P. G. power and opportunity to act), that the dear Gospel may be received in the principality, and continue there.

For there are many and great secret

enemies among us, who boast themselves great lovers of the Word, and yet, in their hearts, hate those who deliver it; which is a most pernicious and churlish trick, extinguishing the dear Gospel by much and great extolling. May Y. P. G. accept this from me in good part, and graciously. For how can I desist? and how would it become me not to care for the dear Gospel, or to hear any thing to its detriment silently? Herewith, I commend you to the dear God. Amen.

Your Princely Grace's obedient,

MARTINUS LUTHER.

Friday after John the Baptist, 1540.

LETTER XLIII.

To his Wife. July 16, 1540.

Written from Eisenach, where Luther was attending a meeting.

To my gracious Girl, Katherine Luther von Bora and Zulsdorf, at Wittenberg, my darling.

GRACE and peace, my dear girl, and wife Kate. Your Grace must be informed that we all here are—God be praised!—fresh and sound: we eat like behemoths (yet not much), and drink like Germans (yet not much), and are joyous. For our gracious Lord of Magdeburg, Bishop Amsdarf, is our messmate. We have no other news than that D. Caspar, Mecum,[1] and Menius,[2] have made an excursion from Hagenau[3] to Strasburg, to

---

[1] Mecum, or Frederic Myconius, first superintendent at Gotha.

[2] Justus Menius, superintendent at Gotha; died professor at Thomas College, at Leipzig.

[3] At Hagenau there was a religious conference.

I

do honour and service to Hans von Jehnen.[1] M. Philippus is well again,[2] God be praised! Tell my dear D. Schiefer[3] that his King Ferdinand holds forth as though he would invite the Turks to be sponsors for the evangelical Princes.[4] I hope it is not true, for it would be too bad. Write to me again whether you have got all I sent you: that is, 90 fl. by Wolf Paermann, &c. God be with you. Amen. Make the children pray. There is an indescribable and unbearable heat and sterility here, day and night. May the dear last day come soon. Amen. The Bishop of Magdeburg greets you kindly.

Your darling,

MARTIN LUTHER.

Friday after Margaret-
    day, 1540.

[1] Duke John of Saxony.
[2] Philippus was very ill on the journey.
[3] He had been tutor of the Princes at Ferdinand's Court, and dismissed as an adherent of Luther.
[4] A facetious threat.

LETTER XLIV.

To the same.   July 26, 1540.

To the rich lady of Zülsdorf, Frau Doctor Katherine Luther, dwelling in body at Wittenberg, and wandering in spirit to Zülsdorf: to be delivered into the hands of my darling; if absent, to be opened and read by D. Pomeran, Pastor.

PRAY arrange that we may find a good supply of beer with you; for, God willing, we shall be at Wittenberg on Tuesday morning. The Diet at Hagenau is all muck, lost trouble and labour, and useless expense; yet, if we have done nothing more, we have fetched M. Philipp again from hell, and will bring him home again joyfully from the grave, God willing, and by his grace. Amen. The devil here is himself possessed with new bad devils, and burns and does frightful mischief. More than a thousand acres of wood belonging to my gracious lord in the Thuringian wood have been burnt, and are burning. Besides this, we have to-day news that the woods at Werda and in many more places are also destroyed; there is no extinguishing them. That will make wood dear. Pray yourself, and cause others to do so, against the malignant Satan, who seeks vehemently not only our souls and bodies, but our property and honour. May Christ our Lord come from heaven, and blow up a spark for the devil and his associates that he cannot extinguish! Amen. I am not certain whether this letter will find you at Wittenberg or at Zülsdorf, else I would have written more. God be with you. Amen. Greet our children, boarders, and all.

Your darling,
M. LUTHER, D.

Monday after Jacobus, 1540.

LETTER XLV.

To the same.   September 18, 1541.

Katherine was probably at her property at Zülsdorf.

GRACE and peace to you. Dear Kate, I send Urban to you with this, that you may not be frightened if any alarm about the Turks should reach you. I wonder that you have not written or sent, as you well know that we are not without anxiety about you here, as Meinz, Heinz, and many of the nobles at Meissen, are very inimical to us. Dispose of and arrange what you can, and come home; for it appears to me that it will rain mire, and God will visit our sins with the rod of his anger. God be with you. Amen.

M. LUTHER.

Sunday after Lampertus, 1541.

XLVI.

Luther's Will. January 6, 1542.

It was confirmed by the Elector in 1566.

I, MARTIN LUTHER, certify, in this my own handwriting, that I have given to my true and loving wife Katherine, as dowry (or whatever else one may call it), for her whole life, for her pleasure and advantage, and do give her by virtue of this letter at present and this day:

First, the little property of Zülsdorf, as I have bought and arranged it, and in all respects as I have hitherto had it.

Secondly, the house of Bruno, for a dwelling, which I bought under the name of my "Wolf."[1]

Thirdly, the goblets and ornaments, such

---

[1] Luther had bought it of Pastor Bruno, a peasant, under the name of his amanuensis, Wolfgang Sieberger.

as rings, chains and medals, gold and silver, value about 1000 fl.

I do so for these reasons:

First, because she has always loved and esteemed me as her pious, true, and lawful husband, to whom she has borne and reared, through God's abundant blessing, five living children; and God grant they may long continue so.

Secondly, that she may take upon her and pay any debts I have incurred (in case I should not be able to do so during my life), which may be, as far as I know, 450 fl., but may perhaps be found to be more.

Thirdly and chiefly, that I desire the children[1] to look to her for support, not she to the children; and that they may hold her

[1] Luther's children were: 1. John, born June 7, 1526; died at Königsberg, October 28, 1572, Doctor of Law. 2. Elizabeth, born December 10, 1527; died August 3, 1528. 3. Magdalen, born May 4, 1529; died October 20, 1542. 4. Martin, born November 7, 1531; died March 3, 1565. 5. Paulus, born January 28, 1533; died March 8, 1593, physician. 6. Margaret, born December 16, 1534, wife of the Herr von Kunheim; died 1570.

in honour, and be subject to her, as God has commanded. For I have truly seen and experienced how the devil excites and provokes children against this law, even when they are good, through malicious and envious gabblers, especially when the mothers are widows, and the sons get wives, and the daughters husbands; and again, *socrus nurum, nurus socrum.* For I consider that the mother will be the best guardian to her own children, and will make use of such dowry and property, not to the injury and detriment of the children, 'but for their use and advantage; for they are her own flesh and blood, and she has borne them under her heart.

And though she should be necessitated or find reason (for I can place no limit to the works and will of God) to change her state, yet I trust and have perfect confidence that she will demean herself as a mother to all her children, and divide all faithfully, be it dowry or aught else, as is right.

And I herewith submissively beg of the high and mighty lord, Duke John Frederic,

Elector, &c., that H. P. G. will maintain and protect all such gifts or dowries.

I also beg of all my good friends that they will be witnesses for my dear Kate, and help to exculpate her if gossiping tongues should molest or calumniate her, as though she kept back certain ready money which she would embezzle or purloin from the poor children. I bear witness that there is no ready money, but only the goblets and jewels mentioned above in the dowry. And, indeed, the reckoning may be publicly made by every one, because it is known how much income I have received from my high and mighty lord, and beyond that, not a penny; nor have we received a mite from any one, except such presents as are mentioned above among the jewels, or the portion which is put down as debt. And that, with such an income and presents, I should have been able to afford to build and buy so much, and maintain so large and heavy a household expenditure, I consider as a special and wonderful blessing, and that it is no wonder that I have left no ready money, but rather debts. This therefore I beg; for the devil, though he could not come nigh to me, might in all ways seek after my Kate, if only for the reason that she has been the wedded wife of the man D. M., and, God be praised, is so still.

Lastly, I beg of every one, as in this gift or dowry I have not used legal forms or words (for which I have had reasons), to allow me to be the person, which in truth I am, known both in heaven and earth, and also in hell, of sufficient consideration and authority to be trusted more than any notary. For if God, the Father of all mercy, has intrusted to me, a poor, unworthy, miserable sinner, the Gospel of his dear Son, and has likewise made me faithful, and true therein, and has hitherto found and kept me thus,—so that many have accepted the same through me, and consider me a teacher of truth, in spite of the Pope's law, and the wrath of the emperor, kings, princes, priests, nay, of all devils,—shall I not much more be believed in this so small a matter, especially as here is my handwriting, so well known; therefore I hope it will be sufficient when it can be shown and said, This is the earnest and well-considered intention of D. M. L. (God's notary, and witness of his Gospel), done by his own hand and seal.

M. L.

Witnessed by Melancthon, Cruciger, and Bugenhagen.

Done and given on the day of Epiphany, 1542.

LETTER XLVII.

To the Widow of J. Cellarius.[1]
May 8, 1542.

Letter of consolation.

GRACE to you, and peace in Christ, honourable, virtuous, and dear lady. I have with sorrow learnt how God the dear Father has chastised you and us also with his rod, in taking away from you and us the dear man Johann Cellarius, your husband, which is a grief to us all, though he is in happy, blissful rest. But be comforted by this,—that your sorrow is not the greatest experienced by the children of men; there are many who suffer and endure a hundred times more. And if all our sufferings on earth were piled up in a heap, they would be as nothing compared with what the guiltless Son of God has suffered for us and our salvation; for no death can

---

[1] Professor of Hebrew at Leipzig.

be compared with the death of our Lord and Saviour Christ, through whose death we are all saved from eternal death.

Be therefore comforted in the Lord, who has died for you and all, and is worth more than we men, women, and children, and all are; for we are his, whether we die or live, are rich or poor, or however it may be. And if we are his, He also is ours, with all that He is and has. Amen. I commend you to his grace. My Kate sends you comfort in God.

Monday after Cantate, 1542.

LETTER XLVIII.

To one unknown.   January 11, 1543.

To give peace of conscience.

GRACE and peace in the Lord. My dear Frau Margarita, your brother Johannes has informed me how your heart is troubled by the Evil Spirit, whereby you have uttered such wicked words. I would that the devil would fetch away all those who have so advised you, that thus he may torment and prompt you, as if you were to remain eternally his.

Ah, dear Margarita, as you feel and confess that it is the Evil Spirit who has dragged such words from you, and that it is his wicked suggestion, be assured that all he suggests are lies; as "he is a liar, and the father of lies" (John viii. 44). For assuredly it is not suggested by Christ that you should belong to the devil, seeing that He has died that those who are under the power of the devil may be released from him. Therefore do thus to the devil: spit at him, and say, "Have I sinned? Alas! I have sinned, and it grieves me; but I will not despair; for Christ has borne and taken away all my sins—nay, those of the whole world, if they only confess their sins, amend, and believe in Christ, who commanded 'that repentance and remission of sins should be preached in his name among all nations' (Luke xxiv. 4). And what should I do if I had committed murder, adultery—nay, had crucified Christ Himself? yet would it be forgiven, according to his prayer upon the cross—'Father, forgive them.' This I am bound to believe, and am also absolved; therefore, avaunt thee, devil! for ever away!"

Thus shall you, dear Margarita, not believe in the devil nor your own thoughts; but in us preachers, whom God has commanded to instruct souls, comfort and absolve them, as He says (Matt. xvi. 19; John xx. 23): "Whosesoever sins ye remit, they shall be remitted." This you should believe, and not doubt. Now we preachers absolve and free you, in Christ's name and by his command, not only from this one sin, but from all the sins born in you from Adam; which are so many and great, that God in his goodness will not let us see them all and entirely, nor feel them thoroughly (for we could not bear it), still less reckon them against us, if we believe in Him.

Therefore be content and comforted; your sins are forgiven you. Rest boldly on this; do not turn again to your thoughts, but listen only to what your pastor and preacher tell you from God's Word; do not despise their word and comfort,—for it is Christ Himself who speaks to you through them; as He says, "He that heareth you heareth Me" (Luke x. 16). Believe this, and the devil will away, and leave you. But if you are still weak in faith, say thus: "I would willingly be firmer in my faith, and I know well that these things are true and to be believed. Though now I am not sufficiently firm in faith, yet I know that it is the pure truth." That is called "believing unto righteousness" and salvation; as Christ says (Matt. v. 6): "Blessed are they who hunger and thirst after righteousness."

Christ our dear Lord, who was delivered for our offences, and was raised again for our justification (Rom. iv. 25), comfort and strengthen your heart in true faith; and be not troubled concerning your sins.

D. MARTINUS LUTHER.

Thursday after Epiphany, 1543.

LETTER XLIX.

To the Electress Elizabeth of Brandenburg.
October 22, 1543.

Concerning a preacher's appointment.

To the most Serene and High-born Princess and Lady, Frau Elizabeth, born of the royal race of Denmark, Electress of Brandenburg, Duchess of Stettin, Pomerania, Wittwen, &c., my most gracious lady and dear godmother.

GRACE and peace in the Lord. Most serene and high-born Princess, most gracious Lady, &c.; according to the desire of Y. E. P. G., I will diligently urge upon the Visitors that they shall place another preacher at Prettin, in the room of Johann Fabri, whom Y. E. P. G. has called to be court preacher, if the Pastor Severin retires. I heard yesterday that he refuses to go to Pelgern. But that will soon be known. Herewith, God be with you. Amen.

Your Electoral Princely Grace's obedient,
MARTINUS LUTHER, D.

Monday after Lucii, 1543.

LETTER L.

To the same. February 10, 1544.

Thanks for the fulfilment of a request.

To the most Serene, High-born Princess and Lady, Frau Elizabeth, born of the royal race of Denmark, Margravine of Brandenburg, Electress of Wittwen, my gracious lady and godmother.

GRACE and peace. Most serene, high-born Princess, most gracious Lady, and dear Godmother; I have learnt with hearty gladness, from Y. E. P. G.'s letter, that you will quite willingly—nay, even graciously—permit Herr Johann Faber to be pastor in the town of Prettin. Y. E. P. G. will thus have done a good work; for, as he has been known there before, and will be thankfully welcomed, I hope much fruit may be produced, and God give it his blessing. I am bound and willing to serve Y. E. P. G.

The dear God and Father of our Lord and Saviour Jesus Christ be with your Electoral Princely Grace always. Amen.

MARTINUS LUTHER.

Sunday after Dorothea, 1544.

LETTER LI.

To the Electress Sibylla of Saxony.
March 30, 1544.

A letter of thanks and consolation.

To the most Serene, High-born Princess and Lady, Frau Sibylla, born Duchess of Jules and Cleves, &c., Duchess of Saxony, Electress, Landgravine of Thuringia, Margravine of Meissen, and Burgravine of Magdeburg, my gracious lady.

GRACE and peace in the Lord. Most serene, high-born Princess, I thank Y. E. P. G. quite humbly that you have so anxiously and constantly inquired after my health, and how it fares with my wife and children, wishing me also all happiness. It fares well with us, God be praised, and better than we deserve in the sight of God. That my head, however, is not sometimes very strong is no wonder. Old age is there, which in itself is old and cold, ill-fashioned, sick, and weak. The pitcher continues to go for water, till at last it breaks.

I have lived long enough. God grant me a happy closing hour, wherein this corrupt, vile body shall go under the earth to its kindred, and become the portion of worms. I consider also that I have seen the best that I can see on earth; for it seems as if things would become worse. God help his own! Amen. When Y. E. P. G. tells me how wearisome it is to you that our gracious Lord, Y. E. P. G.'s husband, should be absent, I can well believe it; but as it is needful, and such absence is for the advantage and good of the German nation and Christendom, we must bear it with patience, according to God's will.[1] If the devil could keep quiet, we should have more peace, and less to do, and not suffer so much annoyance. But we have the advantage of possessing the dear Word of God, which comforts and supports us in this life, and promises and brings us to the future life of bliss. We have also prayer, which we know (as Y. E. P. G. writes) is pleasing to God, and will be heard by Him in his good time. These two unspeakable treasures neither the devil,

---

[1] The Elector was at the Diet of Spires.

nor the Turk, nor the Pope, nor any of his, can have, and are therefore far poorer and more miserable than any beggar on earth. We may assuredly boast and comfort ourselves, and thank God, the Father of all mercy, in Christ Jesus his dear Son our Lord, that He has granted us such a dear and holy treasure, and appointed for us unworthy, such a jewel, through his abundant grace; that we therefore should not only willingly and gladly see and suffer the evils of this world, but also have compassion on the blind, miserable world, and especially on its great leaders, that they are deprived of such grace, and not yet found worthy of it. May God in time enlighten them, that they also may, with us, see, discern, and comprehend it! Amen. My Kate begs to offer her poor prayers for Y. E. P. G., and in all humility thanks Y. E. P. G. for so graciously thinking of her. Herewith, God be with you. Amen.

Your Electoral Princely Grace's humble,
MART. LUTHER, D.

Judica, 1544.

LETTER LII.

To the same. April 28, 1544.

To the most Serene, High-born Princess and Lady, the Frau Sibylla, born Duchess of Jülich, &c., Duchess of Saxony, Electress, Landgravine of Thuringia, Margravine of Meissen, and Burgravine of Magdeburg, my gracious lady.

GRACE and peace, and my poor Pr. Nr. Most serene, high-born Princess and gracious Lady, Dr. Augustin has addressed me on behalf of Y. E. P. G., about the answer that I was to write to Y. E. P. G.'s letter. But I hope that my answer has meanwhile come to Dr. Augustin, with Y. E. P. G.; for I sent it by Captain Asmus Spiegel,[1] because I had not, and knew not, of any other messenger. If it so happens that they should not have come to Y. E. P. G., I will willingly answer again. For I have heartily thanked, and do still thank, Y. E. P. G. for your gracious letter and favour.

[1] Erasmus Spiegel, Captain at Wittenberg.

We hope and pray that God will send home our dear sovereign and most gracious lord speedily and joyfully. Amen. There is not much to be done now with the **Papists**, without their consuming us with expenses, and emptying our purses, although they pretend that they are willing, and yet are not. May our Lord Jesus, whose work it is, and who has begun it, bring it Himself to an end, as He will do, and has hitherto done; otherwise it will remain undone, and nothing good will come of it. To Him, in his mercy, I commend Y. E. P. G., together with the dear ladies, &c. Amen.

Your Electoral Princely Grace's humble,

M. LUTHER, D.

Monday, Vitalis, 1544.

LETTER LIII.

To the Wife of Jerome Baumgärtner,[1] at Nuremberg. July 8, 1544.

Letter of consolation.

GRACE to you, and peace in our dear Saviour and Lord Jesus Christ. Honourable, virtuous, and dear lady, God, who sees and hears my sighs, knows how heartfelt is my sorrow for your grief and misfortune; indeed, every one is heartily grieved for the dear man who has so sadly fallen into the hands of the enemy. May God hear our prayer, and that of all pious hearts! For it is certain that all pious hearts pray earnestly for him; and assuredly such prayers will be acceptable and agreeable to God.

Meanwhile, we must comfort ourselves with the divine promises, that He will not

---

[1] Jerome Baumgärtner, a senator of Nuremberg, had been taken prisoner by one of the Franconian Knights, Von Rosenberg.

abandon or forget those who are his, with which the Psalter abounds; for we know that your lord is an upright man in the faith of Christ, which he has worthily confessed, and adorned by many fine fruits. Therefore it is impossible that He should have cast him off; but, as He has called him through his Holy Word to Himself, and received him into his gracious bosom, He will keep him evermore in that bosom, and will daily support him. It is the same God who has, before this misfortune, kept him as his dear Christian and child of life. He will remain the same God to him, though He may appear otherwise for a short time, in order to try our faith and patience a little. He has said (in John xvi. 20, 22): "Ye shall be sorrowful; but your sorrow shall be turned into joy, which no man taketh from you." This his promise He will keep without fail.

Besides, our sufferings are not so great and bitter as were those of his dear Son, and his dear mother, which should comfort and strengthen us in our sorrows; as St. Peter teaches us (1 Pet. iii. 18): "For Christ also hath once suffered for sins, the just for the unjust." The devil and his rejoice in our misfortunes, but shall bitterly enough lament that they have so done; and their short joy shall become a long mourning. But we have the glorious and great advantage, that God is merciful and gracious to us, with all angels and creatures; therefore, no misfortunes of this body can injure the soul, but rather are useful to us; as St. Paul says (Rom. viii. 28): "We know that all things work together for good to them that love God." In respect to the body, we suffer woe, and shall and must do so; for we should not be true Christians did we not suffer with Christ, and had not sympathy with sufferers.

Therefore, my dear lady, suffer and be patient; for you do not suffer alone, but have many, many excellent, faithful, pious hearts, who have great sympathy with you, who all do according to the saying (Matt. xxv. 36): "I was in prison, and ye came unto Me." Yea, truly, in great crowds we visit the dear Baumgärtner in his prison, that is, the Lord Christ Himself, imprisoned in the person of a true member; and we pray and call upon Him to liberate him, and thus gladden the hearts of you and all of us. May the same Lord Jesus, who calls upon us to comfort one another, and comforts us by his Holy Word, comfort and strengthen your heart by his Spirit, in steadfast patience, until the happy end of this and all misfortunes. To whom, together with the Father and Holy Spirit, be honour and praise for ever. Amen.

MARTINUS LUTHER, D.

*Tuesday after the Visitation
of Mary,* 1544.

LETTER LIV.

To Frau Jörger.   July 13, 1544.

Account of her Nephews.

GRACE to you, and peace in the Lord. Honourable and virtuous lady, we have received your dear nephews and children, and hope that they will be honourably and well taken care of by the pious Magister George Meyer. God grant them grace, that they may study well, and become pious, as I have good hope in them. For in these bad times it is needful that there should be many pious people, who will help us, by their good lives and prayers, to expiate our former and daily increasing sins, and to turn away the chastisement which is ready to fall on our heads. For the former idolatry of the Papacy (which they will not yet give up), and our ingratitude, press heavily upon us. May the merciful God follow after us with his Holy

Spirit, and graciously perfect the good work He has begun in us through his Holy Word! Amen. To whose grace I commend you; and pray for a blessed, short end for me, for it is well nigh the time for my journey home, and rest.

D. MARTINUS LUTHER.

Datum die Margarethæ,
    1544.

LETTER LV.

To the same. September 5, 1544.

Letter of consolation.

To the honourable and virtuous Lady, Dorothea Jörger, widow, at Kappach, my well-wisher and friend.

GRACE and peace in the Lord. Honourable, virtuous, and dear lady, with respect to your nephews, I expect that their preceptor, M. George Meyer, will have written to you all the circumstances. I can well believe that you are grieved at the disunion of your sons; and I am truly sorry, both for their discord and your trouble. Now, what is to be done? There must be misfortunes and crosses in this life; by these God drives us to his Word and prayer, that He may hear and comfort us. Therefore, do not desist from admonishing them, by God's Word, to brotherly love; and likewise earnestly pray, that God may prosper and further with his grace such admonitions, as He has commanded us to pray and to trust in Him: "Ask, and it shall be given you; seek, and you shall find; knock, and it shall be opened to you." I would have written to them now; but, as they might suspect that I had been informed by you, I will refrain till I can say, "I have learnt it from others;" and then I will represent, as sharply as I can, what a bad example they set; and God grant his blessing. Amen. My Kate and children thank you kindly for your greeting and good-will. Herewith, God be with you. Amen.

       MARTINUS LUTHER.

September 5, 1544.

LETTER LVI.

To the Widow of George Schulzen.
October 8, 1544.

Letter of consolation.

GRACE to you, and peace in the Lord. Honourable and virtuous Frau Heva, and good friend, I am grieved at your misfortune, God having taken your dear husband from you. I can well believe the pain of such a parting; it would not be well if it did not give you pain, for it would be a sign of cold love.

But, on the other hand, you may have great comfort: First, because his departure hence was Christian and blessed. Secondly, because the will of God, our dear Father, is altogether best: who gave his Son for us. How fitting, then, is it that we should sacrifice our will to his, for his service and pleasure, which is not only our duty, but from which we have much fruit and joy!

But may He, our dear Lord Jesus Christ, comfort you abundantly by his Spirit! Amen. Herewith, I commend you to the dear God.

Wednesday after Franciscus, 1544.

LETTER LVII.

To an Aged Couple.   October 25, 1544.

On the death of their son.

GRACE to you, and peace in Christ, our Lord and Saviour. Honourable, dear, good friends, the preceptor of your dear son of blessed memory has begged me to write this letter, and advise you in the misfortune which, as parents, you have experienced in the death of your son. And truly it is not to be believed that you should not be sorry; it would indeed not be a nice thing to hear that father and mother were not grieved at the death of their son. So says also the wise man, Jesus Sirach, chap. xxii. 10, 11 : " Thou shalt mourn over the dead, for his light is extinguished; yet shall you not mourn much, for he is gone to his rest."

And thus you, when you have sorrowed and wept moderately, shall comfort yourselves again,—nay, thank God with joy that your son has made such a good end, and has gone to sleep so softly in Christ, that there can be no doubt that he must be sleeping sweetly and softly in the eternal rest of Christ. For every one is amazed at this great mercy, that he has continued steadfast to the end in prayers and confession of Christ, which grace should be more acceptable to you than if he had flourished a thousand years in all this world's good things and honours. He has taken with him the greatest treasure he could attain to in this life.

Therefore be comforted; he is well off in comparison of many thousands who perish miserably—nay, sometimes dishonourably—and die in their sins. Therefore it were heartily to be desired that you and all yours, together with all of us, should, through God's grace, so depart. He has conquered the world and the devil, whilst we are still daily liable to be overcome, and must be exposed to all the dangers against which he is now secure. You sent him to the right school, and applied well your love and care. God help us also hereafter. Amen.

May the Lord and most high Comforter Jesus Christ—who has loved your son better than yourself, having first called him through his Word, and afterwards summoned him to Himself, and taken him from you—comfort and strengthen you with his grace, till the day when you will see your son again in eternal joy! Amen.

MARTINUS LUTHER, D.

Saturday after St. Lucas, 1544.

LETTER LVIII.

To his Wife.   July 1545.

Written from Leipzig, where Luther had gone with his sons, from dissatisfaction at the prevailing corruption of morals at Wittenberg.

GRACE and peace to you. Hans will tell you every thing concerning our journey. I am, however, not yet certain whether he shall remain with me; but D. Caspar Cruciger and Ferdinand will tell you. Ernst von Schönfeld entertained us well at Lobnitz, and Heinz Scherle still better at Leipzig.[1] I would gladly arrange so that I need not return to Wittenberg. My heart is chilled, so that I would not willingly stay there; and I wish that you would sell the garden and land, house and farm; then I will give back the large house to M. G. H. And it would be best for you to establish yourself at Zülsdorf, whilst I am still alive, and can help you with

[1] A merchant in Leipzig.

my salary to improve the property; for I hope that M. G. H. will continue to me the salary,—at least to the last year of my life. After my death you will not be able to bear the four elements at Wittenberg; therefore it would be better to do what has to be done during my life. Perhaps Wittenberg, with its government, as it would seem, will get not St. Vitus's nor St. John's dance, but the beggars' or Beelzebub's, as they have begun: and there is no one there to control or punish; and God's Word will be derided. Away, then, from this Sodom! I have heard more in the country than I learnt in Wittenberg; therefore I am weary of the city, and will not, so God help me, return there. The day after to-morrow I travel to Merseburg, Prince George having much begged of me to do so. I will stroll about and eat beggar's bread rather than torment and disturb my poor last days with the disorderly life at Wittenberg, and witness the loss of all my hard, precious work. You may, if you like, let Dr. Pommer and Mag. Philippus know this; and perhaps Dr. Pommer will give my good-by to Wittenberg, for I am bursting with anger and disgust. Herewith, God be with you. Amen.

MARTINUS LUTHER.

Tuesday after Whitsuntide, 1545.

LETTER LIX.

To the same.   January 25, 1546.

Luther is on a journey to Eisleben, to arrange the disputes betwixt the Counts of Mansfeld.

To be delivered to my dear Kate Luther,
at Wittenberg.

GRACE and peace in the Lord. Dear Kate, we arrived to-day, about eight o'clock, at Halle, but did not go on to Eisleben; for a great Anabaptist met us, with billows of water and blocks of ice, which covered the country, and threatened to baptise us again. Nor could we return, on account of the Mulda; so we are obliged to remain quietly at Halle, betwixt the two waters,—not that we thirst for it to drink, but refresh and comfort ourselves with good Torgau beer and Rhine wine, until the Saal have ceased raging. For, as the servants, ferrymen, and we ourselves were alarmed, we would not trust ourselves to the water, and tempt God, as the devil is furious with us, and dwells in the water-floods; and prevention is better than cure; nor is it necessary to make ourselves a laughing-stock to the Pope and his fellows. I should not have thought that the Saal could have made such a bubbling, and burst in this way over the causeway and all.

No more now; but pray for us, and be pious. I hold that, had you been here, you would have advised us to do the same; and thus we should for once have followed your advice. Herewith, God be with you. Amen.

MARTINUS LUTHER, D.

At Halle, on the day of the Conversion of St. Paul, 1546.

LETTER LX.

To the same. February 1, 1546.

Written from Eisleben.

To my heartily beloved wife Katherine Luther, Zulsdorfian Doctoress,[1] swine-marketian, and whatever else she may be.

GRACE and peace in Christ, and my old poor love, as before. Dear Kate, I became very weak on the road before reaching Eisleben, for my sins. But if you had been there, you would have said it was for the sins of the Jews; for we had to pass through a village a little way from Eisleben where many Jews dwell, and perhaps they have blown cold upon me. There are now here in the city of Eisleben above fifty Jews residing; and it is true that when I passed through the village, such a cold wind came from behind the carriage on to my head through my cap, as

[1] Evidently an expression of contempt for Wittenberg.

though it would turn my brain to ice. This may have helped to cause my dizziness; but I am now, thank God, stronger.

When the main business is settled, I will take steps to drive away the Jews. Count Albrecht hates and no longer protects them; but no one yet does aught against them. Please God, I will help Count Albrecht in the pulpit, and leave them to their fate likewise.

Your sons left Mansfeld yesterday, as Hans von Jene had so humbly prayed they would. I know not what they are doing there. If it were cold, they might help me to shiver here; but now it is warm, they may do or suffer what else pleases them. Herewith, God be with you, and all the household; and greet all our friends.

M. L., YOUR OLD DARLING.

Vigilia Purificationis, 1546.

LETTER LXI.

To the same.   February 6, 1546.

From the same place.

To the deeply-learned lady Katherine Luther, my gracious wife, at Wittenberg.

GRACE and peace. Dear Kate, we sit here, and let ourselves be tormented, and would gladly be away; but that cannot be, I think, for a week. Tell Magister Philipp that he may correct his exposition; for he has not understood why the Lord in the Gospel calls riches thorns. Here is the school where one may learn to understand it.[1] But it dawns on me why, in the Holy Scriptures, the thorns are always threatened with fire; therefore I wait with greater patience, that, by God's help, I may bring matters to a good end. Your sons are still at Mansfeld. I have plenty to eat and drink, and might have

[1] Luther alludes here to the disputes he had to settle.

pleasant days, if this vexatious quarrel were settled. It appears to me that the devil scoffs at us; but God will laugh him to scorn. Amen. Pray for us. The messenger is in great haste.

MARTINUS LUTHER, D.

On St. Dorothy's-day, 1546.

LETTER LXII.

To the same.   February 7, 1546.

From the same place.

To my dear wife Katherine Luther, doctoress and self-tormentor, at Wittenberg; to the hands and feet of my gracious lady.

GRACE and peace in the Lord. Read, dear Kate, St. John and the small catechism, of which you sometimes say, all in this book is said of me. For you must needs take God's cares on you, just as if He were not Almighty, who could create ten Doctor Martinus's, if the one old one were drowned in the Saal, or at Ofenloch, or at Wolf's Vogelheerd.[1] Leave me in peace with your cares; I have a better guardian than you and all the angels—He who lay in a manger, and hung on a virgin's breast, but now sits at the right

[1] Probably allusions to particular places.

hand of the Almighty Father. Therefore be in peace. Amen.

I think that hell and the whole world must be empty of all their devils, who perhaps have all met together on my account at Eisleben, so stiff and stubborn is the state of affairs. There are Jews here, near fifty in a house, as I have before written to you. They say that at Rissdorf, near Eisleben, the place where I was ill on my journey hither, nigh four hundred Jews pass in and out. Count Albrecht, to whom all the frontier round Eisleben belongs, has withdrawn his protection from any Jews who may be seized on his property; yet no one will as yet do any thing to them. The Countess of Mansfeld, widow of Solms, is considered the protector of the Jews. I know not whether it is true; but I have made it strongly enough apparent to-day, if one chooses to understand it, what my opinion is, if it is of any use. Pray, pray, pray, and help us, that we may do it well. For to-day I had a mind to give full vent to my wrath, but was restrained when the wretchedness of my fatherland occurred to me. I have become a lawyer also now; but it will not answer to them. They had better have let me remain a theologian. If I were to come among them, if I should live, I might become an ogre, who would, by God's grace, check their pride. They give themselves airs, as though they were God, from which they had better desist in time, before their godhead becomes devildom, as happened to Lucifer, who could not remain in heaven on account of his pride. Well, God's will be done. Let M. Philipp read this letter; for I have not time to write to him. We live well here, and the Councillor sends me every day, at meal-time, a half-stoup of Rheinfall, which is very good. I sometimes drink it with my friends. The wine of the country also is very good here, as is likewise the Naumburg beer, except that it seems to make me very phlegmatic with its pitch. The devil has spoilt the beer all over the world with his pitch, and the wine about you with brimstone. But here there is pure wine, excepting that of the country. Know that all the letters you have written have come here, and to-day the one which you wrote last Friday, with M. Philipp's letter. I mention this, that you may not be angry.

    Your dear lord,
       M. LUTHER.

The Sunday after St. Dorothy's-day, 1546.

LETTER LXIII.

To the same. February 10, 1546.

From the same place.

To the saintly, anxious-minded lady Katherine Luther, Doctoress and Zulesdorferin, at Wittenberg, my gracious and dear wife.

GRACE and peace in Christ. Most saintly Lady Doctoress, we thank you kindly for your great anxiety, which has hindered you from sleeping; for since the time that you have had this care for us, a fire in our inn, close to my chamber-door, has well-nigh consumed us; and yesterday (without doubt through the power of your care) a stone almost fell on our heads, and crushed us, as in a mouse-trap. For in our private chamber, during two days, lime and mortar rattled over our heads, till we sent for workmen, who, touching the stone—which was the size of a large pillow, and two hands'-breadth wide—with two fingers, it fell down. For this we should have had to thank your saintly care, if the dear holy angels had not guarded us. I am anxious lest, if you do not cease to be so anxious, the earth may at last swallow us up, and all the elements persecute us. Do you thus teach the catechism and belief? Pray, and leave it to God to care, as is promised: "Cast thy burden upon the Lord, and He shall sustain thee" (Ps. lv., and in many other places).

We are now, thank God, fresh and sound, except that the state of affairs gives us annoyance; and Dr. Jonas is pleased to have a bad leg, having accidentally knocked himself against a chest: such great envy is there in people, that he would not permit me to have a bad leg alone. Herewith, God be with you. We would now willingly be free and journey home, God willing. Amen, Amen, Amen.

Your Holiness's devoted servant,
MARTINUS LUTHER.

On Scholastica's-day, 1546.

LETTER LXIV.

To the same.   February 14, 1546.

LAST LETTER.

*To my kind, dear wife Katherine Luther von Bora,
at Wittenberg.*

GRACE and peace in the Lord. Dear Kate, we hope, God willing, to return home this week. God has shown us great grace here; for the lords have arranged almost all through their councillors, except two or three articles, among which is, that the two brothers Count Gebhard and Count Albrecht shall become brothers again, which I take in hand to-day, and will invite them to be my guests, that they may speak to one another; for hitherto they have been dumb, and have embittered each other with severe letters. The young men are in good spirits, and make excursions with fool's bells on sledges, accompanied by the ladies; and they masquerade together and are merry, and among them Count Gebhard's son. Thus one must understand that God is *exauditor precum.*[1]

I send you trout, which Countess Albrecht has given me, who is glad at heart at the concord. Your sons are still at Mansfeld; Jacob Luther will take good care of them. We eat and drink here like lords, and we are well waited upon—indeed, too well; so that we might have forgotten you at Wittenberg.

D. Jonas's leg nearly became very bad; but there has been nothing worse than wounds on the shin; but God will help.

You may show all this to M. Philipp, D. Pommer, and D. Cruciger. A report has reached here that D. Martinus has been carried off, as they say, at Leipzig and at Magdeburg. Such are the fictions of your wiseacres of country people. Some say that the Emperor is thirty miles from hence, near Soest, in Westphalia; others, that the French are enlisting, and the Landgrave also. But

---

[1] Hearer of prayer.

let people say as they list; we will await what God will do. Herewith, God be with you.

M. LUTHER, D.

At Eisleben,
on the Sunday Valentine, 1546.

THE END.

LONDON:
LEVEY AND CO., PRINTERS, GREAT NEW STREET,
FETTER LANE, E.C.

www.ingramcontent.com/pod-product-compliance
Lightning Source LLC
Chambersburg PA
CBHW032157160426
43197CB00008B/949